# ACCIDENTS IN NORTH AMERICAN MOUNTAINEERING

## VOLUME 10 • NUMBER 4 • ISSUE 62
### 2009

THE AMERICAN ALPINE CLUB
GOLDEN, CO

THE ALPINE CLUB OF CANADA
BANFF, ALBERTA

ISSN: 0065-082X
ISBN 13: 978-1-933056-09-8

Manufactured in the United States

Published by:
The American Alpine Club
710 Tenth Street, Suite 100
Golden, CO 80401
www.americanalpineclub.org

Cover Illustrations
*Front:* Climbing ranger Matt Hendrickson investigates the exposed ice of a late season crevasse on the Emmons Glacier while descending from a summit patrol on Mount Rainier. Photograph by Mike Gauthier, Climbing Ranger, Mount Rainier National Park.

*Back:* "Three of us, I think, were wandering about up alongside the Diamond for reasons I can't remember and, on a lark, decided to go have a taste. The picture is of John Rensberger, contemplating what was then the unthinkable. When we got back to the ranger station later that day, a sign had been posted saying the Diamond was off-limits to climbing. That lasted for about six years until permission was granted and Bob Kamps and Dave Rearick made the first ascent." Photograph and comment by Tom Hornbein in 1955.

# CONTENTS

SAFETY ADVISORY COUNCIL 2008

**The American Alpine Club**
Aram Attarian, John Dill, Mike Gauthier, Chris Harder, Daryl Miller, Jeff Sheetz, and John E. (Jed) Williamson (Chair)

# ACCIDENTS IN
# NORTH AMERICAN MOUNTAINEERING
Sixty-Second Annual Report of the American Alpine Club

This is the sixty-second issue of *Accidents in North American Mountaineering.*

**Canada:** At the time of publication, narratives and data from Canada were not available. The Alpine Club of Canada has recently secured a new editor for the Canadian content and a resumed regular contribution to Accidents in North American Mountaineering is expected next year. Accident reporting and additional information regarding the 2008 data can be viewed at http://www.alpineclubofcanada.ca/

**United States:** Please notice that we have changed the name of the American Alpine Club Safety Committee to the Safety Advisory Council. The members of the council have never really met as a committee, nor does it have any authority to set policy or take action with matters regarding mountain safety. The individuals have agreed to be "advisory" to the Managing Editor, primarily serving as sources of information and submitting reports. The new title more accurately reflects this role.

Two of this year's accidents involved ascending devices. The one in Zion resulted in a fatality when ascenders severed the rope. The one on El Cap in May that could have had the same consequence was an attempt to reach a climbing partner who had fallen. As John Dill pointed out in this instance, the climber "...did not know what remained to catch him if the top piece pulled, and in a hard fall, his ascenders could have damaged or severed his rope. As he had never had to rescue someone before and didn't know what else to do, he figured that if the top piece had held his partner's fall it should be good for jugging." We continue to see many reports of climbers not being familiar with the intricacies of ascending and belaying devices.

The fatality that occurred on Mount Rainier in June as a result of being stranded due to weather on the Muir Snowfield was counted as a climbing incident even though the party was, technically speaking, hiking. Many people make this ascent to Camp Muir with no problem. However, when the weather changes—and it often does so rapidly—the hikers are suddenly in a mountaineering condition. Often they are not prepared for changing and potentially hazardous conditions. Another kind of incident, not reported in the narratives, occurred when a skier fell 120 feet into a crevasse on the Nisqually Glacier. The party had stopped after skiing for only 15 minutes to evaluate whether they needed to rope up when one of them fell through a snow bridge. The extrication was successful, though the skier was wedged face down. This is a case in which a ski adventure turns into a mountaineering mishap.

As mentioned in previous issues and throughout this report, there are some web-based resources that often provide good information and accident stories. Here is a short-list of some of those sites:

http://home.nps.gov/applications/morningreport/
www.supertopo.com
www.mountainproject.com
http://www.tuckerman.org/
http://www.mountrainierclimbing.blogspot.com/
http://www.friendsofyosar.org/

In addition to the dedicated individuals on the Safety Advisory Council (especially Aram Attarian, who took on Colorado and North Carolina), we are grateful to the following—with apologies for any omissions—for collecting data and for helping with the report: Hank Alacandri, Erik Hansen, Leo Paik, Justin Preisendorfer, Eric White, all individuals who sent in personal stories, and, of course, George Sainsbury.

This year we pay special tribute to Daryl Miller—leader of the South District Rangers in Denali National Park for 18 years. He retired in September. His tireless efforts to educate climbers of all abilities and nationalities and his thoroughness in the reports he sent forward to us all those years are greatly appreciated. For those who have never met him, I recommend going to the climbinglife.com website to read an in-depth story about his life and work.

John E. (Jed) Williamson
Managing Editor
7 River Ridge Road
Hanover, NH 03755
e-mail: jedwmsn@mac.com

# UNITED STATES

## AVALANCHE, POOR POSITION, FAILURE TO TEST CONDITIONS, RELYING ON OTHERS
### Alaska, Delta Range, Castner Glacier

In the early afternoon on March 1, a group of 17 people (15 class members, co-leader Ty Humphrey, and I) arrived on skis and snowshoes in an area with ice cliffs for practicing crevasse rescue in the lower section of the Castner Glacier. I arrived first and found a suitable ice cliff. This ice cliff was located underneath a moraine slope of about 100 feet and the angle of about 35 degrees. The snow on the slope was about thigh deep, mainly sugar snow with a thin slab on top of that.

Being accustomed to the false idea that the moraine slopes on the Castner Glacier are not long enough to accumulate sufficient amount of snow that could create an avalanche of a concerning magnitude, we neglected to give the situation a deeper thought and started setting up anchors at the upper edge of the slope without testing the snow on the slope for stability. The anchors ("dead men" made from skis) were set up in a lower angle (~25 degrees) section of the slope close to the upper edge of the slope and combined with an anchor formed by a rope going around a big rock in a flat area above the slope's edge.

I was the first one to rappel down the slope and the ice cliff. I was just about to unclip from the rope when I heard an avalanche. At first I thought the avalanche was on one of the distant mountain slopes, but it didn't take me too long to figure out that it was actually on the slope above me and coming right on me. Even though I tried to swim, my feet got caught in the packed snow and I got partly buried, with my head, hands, and part of my chest sticking out after the snow movement completely stopped. The only other person affected by the avalanche was Eamon. He was at the upper edge of it when the snow came loose and he ended up riding down with it. After flying down the ice cliff, he supposedly had a relatively soft landing on top of the avalanche debris. Soon after that, Eamon was delivered a shovel and he dug me out from the snow. Nobody was hurt.

Looking at the slope above the ice cliff, it was now pretty much free of snow up to the upper edge of the steep slope section. It ended right below the anchors that were in the lower angle section. The surface was ice and small rocks. The avalanche was most likely triggered by our activity at the upper edge of the steep slope section.

After a short discussion with the class about the mistakes we made, we redid most of the anchors; we placed some of them into the flat area above the slope's edge and made ice-screw anchors on the slope, which now was free of snow and allowed us to find rock-free areas for ice screws. The slope clear of snow and the ice cliff underneath were now safe to practice crevasse rescue. The rest of the course went normally.

## Analysis

My mistake was acting automatically (choosing a similar slope and ice cliff as the last year and the year before) and not using enough thought in action. I should have initiated a snow stability test. Especially since this was a class, we should have spent a good amount of time on analyzing the conditions (pit, layers, compression test, angle estimate, etc.) and reviewed the students' avalanche knowledge.

The mistake of others was not thinking for themselves and relying on my thinking. They should have questioned whether what we were doing was safe. Nobody voiced any concern.

How do we learn from this?

- Prevent acting automatically. Think of what you are doing.
- Be self-sufficient; think for yourself and don't rely on thoughts of others. Safety is everyone's responsibility.
- Even relatively short moraine slopes can pose an avalanche danger. Test the slopes before you use them.

Should we carry beacons on the Castner Crevasse Rescue Course? One of the questions asked by students at the planning meeting before the trip was whether they should have beacons. My answer was that they don't need beacons because we won't be in an avalanche prone area. I encouraged them to have shovels and probes, though (even though at that time I mainly meant it for camping and testing crevasses).

Next time, I still wouldn't require the participants to have beacons, but I would at least recommend them. I think most years we will be able to eliminate avalanche danger by proper selection of ice cliffs to practice on. But good cliffs are scarce and it can sometimes happen that the only suitable ice cliff will have an avalanche slope above it. Beacons could be useful in that situation. I still don't see them as a necessity, though, because we are talking about small avalanches and chances are high that people won't get completely buried and if they do, chances are high that even without beacons they will be quickly found, given the number of people around and given the relatively small area covered by the avalanche. (Source: Tomas Marsik, age unknown)

## HAPE, ALLOWED TO DESCEND ALONE, POSSIBLE CO POISONING
### Alaska, Mount McKinley, West Buttress

The 2008 Ulsam McKinley Expedition, led by Jeong Sang Kim (34) flew onto the glacier on May 1 and climbed to the 14,200-foot camp in eight days. The expedition stayed at the camp waiting for better weather to ascend to the 17,200-foot high camp, and during this time had made at least one carry to the base of the fixed lines at 15,400 feet. The group then made their move to the high camp on May 15. However, Kim felt ill after arriving at the fixed lines and elected to descend while the rest of the expedition continued up. While he was descending solo, he was observed by the NPS patrol stationed at the camp. The patrol noted that he required multiple rest stops while descending and that he could not walk the remaining 200 meters of level ground into the 14,200-foot camp without sitting down twice to rest. The patrol ranger and primary medic contacted Kim, and after a brief physical exam discovered that he had an oxygen saturation of 51 percent, the normal for this altitude being approximately 84 to 89 percent. The one abnormality noted was that pulmonary rales were not found during auscultation. Kim was diagnosed as suffering from atypical High Altitude Pulmonary Edema (HAPE) and brought to the medical tent for treatment. While on low flow oxygen via nasal cannula, his oxygen saturation began to fall to the low 40's. He was immediately placed on high flow oxygen with a non-rebreather mask. Following contact with medical control, he was then administered Diamox and Albuteral. The Incident Command system subsequently was activated and the park helicopter was placed on standby for an evacuation, but poor weather conditions prohibited any evacuation attempt that day. Kim remained in the care of NPS personnel throughout the night and was kept on oxygen. The rest of the Ulsam expedition returned to the 14,200-foot camp the following day and were informed about his condition. Another physical exam was performed to evaluate the possibility of Kim descending with the assistance of his fellow team members, but it was discovered that his saturation level would plummet shortly after being taken off oxygen and not performing any physical exertion. Based on these findings, Kim and another patient were evacuated from the 14,200-foot camp during the evening of May 16 by the NPS Lama helicopter. After being flown to Talkeetna, the two were transferred to a fixed-wing medical evacuation flight for transport to the Alaska Regional Hospital. Kim's symptoms had resolved and he was released following his examination at the hospital.

## Analysis

Kim was fortunate in that the NPS staff suspected that there was something irregular occurring and undertook an investigation. There is a strong possibility that had he gone to sleep alone in his tent that evening, he could have died. Kim's medical condition worsened even after being placed on low flow oxygen and necessitated aggressive medical treatment on the part of the NPS patrol to stabilize him. When I went to consult with the expedition leader, I discovered that while the group was cooking outside the tent, they were using a portable isobutane-style stove to heat the interior. They indicated that this was a normal practice and erroneously stated that since it was a single small stove, there wasn't any danger from it. The expedition had maintained a prudent acclimatization schedule, but the practice of heating their dome tent with a stove put every member at risk of carbon monoxide poisoning and may have contributed to Kim developing HAPE. In addition, splitting the expedition and allowing an ill member to descend by himself could have resulted in Kim's death by the simple fact that no one would have been aware that he was in respiratory distress. Furthermore, un-roped travel on glaciated terrain is not recommended because of the danger of falling into crevasses. (Source: John A. Loomis, Ranger, Denali National Park)

## FROSTBITE – DEHYDRATED, FAILURE TO PAY ATTENTION TO WARNING SIGNS
### Alaska, Mount McKinley, West Buttress

Hervé Laurence (40) was a member of a party of eight French climbers who were planning to ascend via the West Buttress. This group departed on May 6 and purportedly arrived at the 14,200-foot camp on May 12. Following a brief stay for acclimatization the expedition, attempted to climb to the summit in one push. The expedition departed at 0400 on May 16. Laurence reported that his feet were very cold and never warmed up. At 0900, the expedition arrived at Denali Pass. Laurence determined that his hands were now frostbitten and so elected to turn around with one climber. Upon reaching the 17,200-foot camp, the two sought assistance from fellow climbers, who in turn contacted the NPS patrol at 14,200 feet via FRS radio for advice. When questioned, Laurence and his partner stated that they could climb down so they were instructed to continue their descent to 14,200 feet and seek out the rangers upon arrival. The two arrived in camp at1800. A physical exam was performed. Although Laurence was only complaining of frostbite to his hands, a full exam was accomplished and it revealed that Laurence had deep frostbite on the toes of both feet and superficial frostbite on the fingers of both hands. When Laurence was asked why he didn't turn around when his feet began to freeze, he replied that he had suffered frostbite to his feet two times previously and they had always healed without any complications. Further history revealed he had only consumed 1.5 to two liters of water in the previous 48 hours. Following treatment, the patient was evacuated to Talkeetna and then to Anchorage.

### Analysis

This case of frostbite was caused by the climber not hydrating properly and ignoring warning signs. During the climbing briefings conducted by the National Park Service, adequate hydration and the warning signs associated with frostbite are stressed. The climber also stated that he had been wearing mittens when his hands froze. His boots were La Sportiva Olympus Mons, a very popular boot on Denali. At the very least this illustrates that even the best of gear will not necessarily prevent cold injuries and that prevention requires a holistic approach. (Source: John A. Loomis, Ranger, Denali National Park)

## MISSING CLIMBERS – ASSUMED FATAL, INADEQUATE EQUIPMENT – SLEEPING BAGS and FUEL
### Alaska, Mt. McKinley, Cassin Ridge

Tatsuro Yamada (27) and Yuto Inoue (24,) both from Japan, were expected to return from a climb of the Cassin Ridge on May 22. With no sign of the men, the National Park Service began planning the search on May 23, although cloudy and windy weather initially kept all aircraft on standby. From May 24 to May 27, skilled observers flew a total of 33 hours of helicopter and fixed wing flight time in an aerial search effort. More than three thousand high-resolution photos of the search zone were captured during these flights. Analysis of the enlarged and enhanced images enabled a concentrated and effective search effort that continued at ground level after the conclusion of air operations on May 29.

On May 29, in light of the missing climbers limited supplies and the subzero temperatures, search managers concluded that the missing climbers survival was outside the window of possibility. Active field search operations were ceased with no pertinent clues being found to the whereabouts of Yamada and Inoue.

### Analysis

(The following was completed during operations by Daryl Miller, South District Ranger, Denali National Park & Preserve)

This Analysis addresses the practicability of suspending the ongoing Search and Rescue (SAR) activities currently being conducted on and in the vicinity of Mount McKinley from an active air search operation to a complete processing of digital photos. In lieu of the elapsed time since the commencement of SAR operations, the low possibility of survival at this time, and the risk of flying aviation support at high altitude attempting to press forward to increase the probability of detection of the search zone will only place additional personnel at an unwarranted risk.

Specifics:

**1.** Yuto Inoue and Tatsuro Yamada departed Kahiltna Base Camp on May 7 with approximately 5-6 days of food and fuel. They were last seen on May 9 at 7,800 feet on the junction of the North East fork by a French team and an Australian team camped near by intending to climb the West Rib. Since then, the only physical presence of the missing climbers has been tracks on the Kahiltna Peaks and high on the Cassin route. In addition, two sleeping bags and two journals, which were positively identified as belonging to both climbers, was found in their tent at 7,800 feet at the junction of the Northeast Fork.

**2.** Formal SAR activities then commenced on May 23, after the NPS was alerted on May 22 by the Japanese climbers Yusuke Satch, Fumitaka Ichimura, and Katsutaka "Jumbo" Yokoyama of the Giri-Giri #1 expedition. The three Giri-Giri #1 climbers were concerned about their situation on the Cassin, as they reported that Giri-Giri #2 had not returned to their base camp at 7,800 feet on the Northeast Fork of the Kahiltna.

On May 23, the NPS helicopter flew up the Cassin route and over the summit. Recent tracks that appeared to be fresh along with a campsite were seen by Giri-Giri #1 at 17,000 feet after they traversed from the Czech Direct to the Cassin Ridge at 16,000 feet. There were no other climbers that were registered to be on the Cassin Route before this team as well as during their climb time frame. The photos did reveal actual and probable footprints high on the mountain (up to 19,200 feet) and were very instrumental in allowing SAR forces to concentrate their efforts on key areas of the mountain. However, despite clear climatic conditions and two days of examining enhanced photos, no further discoveries of the climbers or their campsites were made.

**3.** The total elapsed time since the start of the climb also brings into question the issue of survivability. As stated, the two climbers had five to six days of food and fuel on the Cassin Route including four cylinders of compressed gas stove fuel for this route. Under optimum conditions one cylinder is good for up to six hours of use before becoming exhausted. On average, one cylinder would be used per day, but if managed correctly, it could be optimistically viewed that two cylinders could be stretched to three days. With this as the baseline, the four cylinders would have been used by the time both climbers reached high on the Cassin. This translates to eight to ten of days of fuel available allowing for the best-case scenario. Food supplies, as opposed to water, would not have as great a bearing on survivability for this short duration of time. Without an adequate fuel source to melt snow into water, climbers will rapidly become dehydrated. Also, with no sleeping bags and a high probability of debilitating frostbite, hypothermia, and fatigue, their chances of survivability will greatly be reduced. Generally a person cannot survive longer than three to four days without consuming fluids at these altitudes. This time period can be extended somewhat by eating snow, but this action hastens an individual's drop into a hypothermic state and further depletes the store of calories available to maintain warmth. Based on these fuel consumption rates, both Climbers would now be on day-ten without being able to acquire the minimum quantity of water necessary to sustain life. The situation is further exacerbated by the extreme cold and dry conditions present on the top of the mountain (as well as not having sleeping bags). In a worst case scenario, fuel would have become exhausted five to six days into the climb, well after both climbers would have been high on the route and in a position where retreat would have been more difficult. In addition, the climbers had pre-positioned a cache at the 14,200-foot camp that was found on May 18 by Giri-Giri #2 with supplies undisturbed. The Giri-Giri#1 team also found the Giri-Giri#2 sleeping bags at the 7,800-foot camp in their tent, suggesting that their situation was even worse and significantly lessens the probability of survival.

**4.** Continuing a high intensity search operation with multiple high-altitude sorties in the absence of any tangible clues as to the general whereabouts of the two climbers exposes rescue personnel to unwarranted risks. Multiple areas of the mountain have been searched by many different aerial resources without success. In addition, the poor prognosis of survival, coupled with the cold temperatures experienced during this period, further justifies that operations be scaled back.

**5.** The aerial search for live persons was officially suspended on May 30. If the bodies of Yuto Inoue and Tatsuro Yamada are discovered, a risk assessment will be conducted before an attempt is made to remove them. Limited search operations should be carried out only if by further examination significant clues are found either by digital photographs or by aviation methods, but only during a period of clear and calm weather.

### Analysis

The known facts make it difficult to comprehend how, after completing the difficult traverse of the Kahiltna Peaks and climbing the most difficult portions of the Cassin, these two talented climbers would run into difficulty on a considerably less technically demanding section of the route. Early May in the Alaska Range is no doubt cold; however, there were not any known significant weather systems that caused problems for any other climbing expeditions high on the mountain in this timeframe.

Though there are many different strategies and styles climbers can employ to undertake the more technically demanding routes, it is critical that all parties carefully consider what equipment can be left behind and what equipment is critical for sustaining the needed strength and stamina for the technically demanding, high altitude, arctic routes of the Alaska Range. (Source: John D. Leonard and Daryl Miller, Rangers, Denali National Park)

### FALL ON ROCK, CLIMBING ALONE
### Alaska, Mount McKinley, West Buttress

Claude Ratté was a member of the Quebecoise 2008 Expedition, which consisted of two party members out of Quebec. Richard Cadorette, the second team member, had left the expedition approximately a week before Ratté's accident due to team dynamic issues that could not be worked out at 14,200 feet. As a result, Ratté continued his climb above 14,200 feet as a solo climber.

At 1159, June 3rd, Ranger Roger Robinson received a call at the Talkeetna Ranger Station from DENA dispatch placed by Claude Ratté from his SAT phone. Ratté said he had fallen off the ridge between 16,200 and 17,200 feet, was not sure of his exact location, and was in his sleeping bag with injuries to his left eye and left ankle.

Ranger Brandon Latham and Dan Escalante (Latham's VIP), stationed at 17,200 feet, received a radio call regarding the incident, then packed and hired the necessary resources for a hasty search down the ridge. Kevin Koprek, a guide with Mountain Trip, was hired as the technical team leader and immediately assembled a team consisting of Brent Okita (Rainer Mountaineering Inc.), Josh O'Halloran (Rainer Mountaineering Inc.), Bill Billmeier (Mountain Trip) and Ted Reckas (private party member). Latham choose Koprek as the Team Leader due to his experience as a Rigging for Rescue instructor and Denali guide. This allowed Latham to focus more on the overall logistics of the operation.

At 1233, Ratté called back to Talkeetna stating he could see the ridge from his location, but was still unsure about where he had fallen from.

Latham prepared equipment from the 17,200-foot cache needed for a long, low angle raising operation, which included one 185m, 9.8mm low stretch rope; two 60m, 9.8mm low stretch ropes; pickets; rock protection (in case the patient was in the rocks below Washburn's Thumb); Sked; anchoring material; tent; stove; food; sleeping bag; and an assortment of medical supplies, including oxygen.

Latham and Escalante (hasty team) went down the ridge to confirm Ratté's location and situation (1255). At this time, Ranger Latham had not received any further information on the location of the patient and had planned on trying to initiate a verbal response through shouting out the patient's name while descending the ridge.

At 1320, Ratté called Talkeetna Ranger Station. The general impression was that he was sounding panicky. He said he felt he may expire in his sleeping bag. He stated he reached the top of the fixed lines and fell to the other side. Latham proceeded down the ridge continuing to shout in hopes for a verbal response upon receiving this new information.

Latham and Escalante arrived at the top of a slope approximately 60 meters above 16,400 feet and received a verbal response to shouts and also had a visual on what was thought to be Ratté's location. Visibility was poor, but Latham was confident they had an idea of Ratté's location and continued to descend to the top of the fixed lines. Meanwhile, Ranger Shain briefed his team at 14,200 feet.

Latham and Koprek's team met at the top of fixed lines to discuss strategies for descending to Ratté's location on Peter's Glacier and conduct a raising operation to the top of the fixed lines. Potential objective hazards were identified and discussed, which included bergschrunds, avalanche hazard, and weather conditions.

At 1354, two teams, led by Latham and Koprek, traveled on 60-meter low stretch ropes with Latham leading down placing pickets for protection. The 600-foot low stretch rope was deployed approximately half way down in order to identify the location for a midway raising station. On the descent, the team encountered two bergschrunds. The first had a three to four foot span, which was relatively easy to navigate through. The second was approximately six to eight feet in height and required a rappel to overcome. The second rope team (Koprek's team) stopped 40 meters above the second bergschrund to establish an anchor in order for Latham, Billmeier, and Escalante to rappel and gain access to the patient. This was accomplished by tying the 600-foot rope and two 200-foot ropes together, which put them in flat terrain 30 feet from Ratté.

Latham and Billmeier reached Ratté at 1540. At this time, Station #1 was re-rigged for a raising operation with a rescue-sized load. Ratté was in stable condition with his chief complaint being pain and swelling in his left ankle and facial trauma. Ratté was packaged in a hypothermia wrap to help maintain a warm and dry environment during transport. Frostbite and increased inter-cranial pressure due to head injuries were two major concerns due to the prolonged exposure to the cold and the lack of movement in the extremities.

The raising operation at station #1 began at 1640. The terrain for the raise ranged from 30-50 degrees and included the two bergschrunds. The patient was switched over from the midway station to the top station. Ratté was then evacuated to the Ranger Camp at 14,200 feet where he was flown out via helicopter to Talkeetna the next day, then transferred to Life Flight to be taken to Anchorage. (Source: Daryl Miller, Ranger, Denali National Park)

*(Editors Note: Maureen McLaughlin, Information Officer, stated the following: From the time of the initial distress call, the entire ground rescue operation took ten-and-a-half hours and involved 14 ground rescuers, including mountaineering rangers, NPS volunteers, mountain guides, and independent climbers. Denali mountaineering staff estimates there have been at least ten significant climbing falls onto the Peters Glacier, including three separate fatalities in 1998. The technical rope rescue of Ratté involves the longest raising operation in Denali mountaineering history.)*

## FALL ON ROCK, UNSAFE POSITION, FATIGUE
### Alaska, Skagway, Black Lake

On June 14, Karl (28) was climbing an unnamed, single-pitch sport route rated at 5.9 near Skagway. Just below the top of the route, he had clipped into the final bolt and was preparing to climb through the crux, where the final bolt was just to the right and above the climber, while the second-last bolt was below and to the left. The crux involved beginning just below a small overhang where the climber under-clings, before climbing above the bolt. Due to the varied surface of this rock, it is natural to place the rope behind one's legs when passing through the crux.

When Karl passed the bolt, he found the natural line to the left of the bolt. The result was that his rope went to the right to the final anchor and back to the left to the second-to-last anchor. At this point, the rope was taut and directly below, passing at 45 degree angle between the anchors. Karl was approximately 1.5 above his final point of protection and three meters above the rope passing between the two anchors.

When Karl fell at the crux, his legs were caught in the rope passing between the anchors, causing him to be thrown upside down. While undesirable, this in itself did not result in any injury. Karl was injured when his foot, caught on the rope, smashed upwards into the overhang.

Karl was lowered to the ground and evacuated to a health centre in Skagway, some 5 km away. He was later diagnosed with a fracture of the left talus.

### Analysis

Karl had noticed from the ground that a previous climber was forced to attempt the crux with the rope behind her legs. He noted that this was un-desirable and potentially dangerous. While at the crux this was confirmed. When Karl arrived at the crux, he was fatigued and did not feel especially strong. Rather than retreating, he attempted the crux knowing he could very well fall and knowing that a fall would be dangerous given the position of the anchors.

The climber should have evaluated his fitness, the configuration of the anchors, and the potential for injury and decided that this move should not have been attempted. Alternatively, Karl could have made a concerted effort to avoid the rope below him while falling. He could have also attempted a different line above the final anchor such that a fall would have avoided the rope. (Source: From a report sent in by Karl)

## FALL INTO BERGSCHRUND, FROSTBITE, WEATHER
### Alaska, Mount McKinley, West Buttress

On the morning of June 16th, climbers woke to clear skies and calm winds at 17,200-foot high camp on the West Buttress. At 0800 as many a three private parties and two guided groups headed out of camp for the summit. At 1300 the weather took a quick turn from clear to obscured skies, winds picked up to 10-15mph, and light snow began to fall. Visibility and winds remained tolerable above Denali Pass (18,200 feet) for all teams to continue their summit push; however, below the pass conditions were much worse. By the time the descending climbers reached Denali Pass, the snow and wind had created a new 5-20cm windslab across the traversing slope that leads from Denali Pass back to High Camp. New snow and whiteout conditions almost completely obscured the poorly marked boot-trail back to camp. All of these factors considerably slowed the downward progress of all the descending teams.

About 0100, Mountain Trip guide Zach Johnson made a FRS radio call to NPS staff at High Camp. He indicated he was unable to find his way back to camp due to poor visibility and asked for assistance. He described their location as somewhere below the traverse from Denali Pass on the upper Peters glacier. NPS staff geared up and began to leave camp when Johnson and a client appeared out of the whiteout having found their own way back to camp.

NPS Ranger Tucker Chenoweth, with the help of AMS guide Leighan Falley and Zach Johnson, left High Camp with a large bundle of wands and headed toward Denali Pass marking the trail as they went to assist the remaining team. A verbal call and response began between descending teams and the NPS team. Descending teams would at times appear from the clouds as if they were floating down the mountain. At 0200 contact was made with Mountain Trip guide Sean McManamy who indicated there were still two rope teams behind him, one of which was having difficulty descending. At this point Johnson joined McManamy and returned to camp to help with their clients. Chenoweth and Falley continued up marking the trail as they went.

About 800 feet above the lower rock band, a team of three climbers was sighted having difficulty descending (Expedition Café Com Leite from Brazil). One member of this team, Cid Vinhate, was having extreme difficulty with the new wind slab and continually lost his footing, almost pulling the other two off their feet. Mittens dangling from his wrist, packed with snow and only glove liners on, Vinhate also had lost his mobility in his hands and could not hold his ice ax. Chenoweth radioed the remaining NPS staff at High Camp for assistance. The NPS team climbed up and short roped Vinhate down to lower angle terrain at the bottom of the traverse. Here they were met by additional staff who escorted them back to camp where they were medically evaluated for altitude and frostbite concerns.

The NPS team moved back up the traverse to contact the only remaining team. About 1000 feet above the lower rock band, the remaining four-person team was spotted. It was decided to wait at the lower rock band and contact them there. Guide Dave Staheli was the third person on a four-person rope team as they descended. As Staheli and his team moved below the rock band, the last client on the rope slipped and fell. Staheli immediately went into self-arrest and was pulled off his stance. Staheli came to rest about 20 feet downhill on an ice bridge, over a bergschrund. His client fell approximately 15 feet into the bergschrund and out of site. The rope was taught and a single picket was holding the weight of the client and Staheli. Chenoweth went down to Staheli and helped him out of the system as Falley fixed and reinforced Staheli's rope. Using another rope, Chenoweth and Staheli built a raising system and hauled the client out of the bergschrund. At 0500 all parties returned to High Camp and after medical assessment, no injuries were found.

At 1200 a reassessment of Vinhate indicated he had minor frostbite to one hand and that the team was fit to descend on their own. Also evaluated was MT-14-Staheli client Mark Howard, who sustained frostbite to two fingers from the tip to the distal knuckle. He was also able to descend with his team. Both were advised to check in with NPS staff at the 14,200-foot camp.

## Analysis

On the morning of June 16th the weather looked promising for a good summit day and teams were lured out. The weather on Denali can change quickly, forcing teams to make difficult and important decisions. These three groups were very high on the mountain as the weather changed, but because the winds and temperatures remained tolerable they continued upward. All teams underestimated the newly snow loaded slopes and the ramifications of the low visibility conditions. Summit day usually takes anywhere from eight to fifteen hours. All teams were slowed down on the decent, the longest day being 20 hours. A day this long creates other problems such as extreme fatigue and increased exposure to weather. Under these conditions one small mistake could mean disaster and often does. Fatigue, difficult slab conditions, and a lack of sufficient wanding on the traverse back to High Camp caused problems for all teams. When the weather changes high on the mountain, it deserves acute attention. On summit day, anything less than a perfect day warrants concern. (Source: Tucker Chenoweth, Ranger, Denali National Park)

## EXPOSURE (TOOK GLOVES OFF) – FROSTBITE
### Alaska, Mount McKinley, West Buttress

KAJ Denali 2008 (from Croatia) expedition members Jadranko Mlinaric (40) and Kristina Marjanovic made a summit attempt on June 27th, turning around at Denali Pass. Mlinaric stated that he removed his gloves for no more than ten minutes. But this resulted in frostbite to all ten fingers. The team then returned to camp at 17,200 feet. On June 29th, an NPS patrol led by Ranger Kevin Wright contacted Mlinaric at 17,200-foot camp and offered assistance and medical help. NPS VIP physician Sven Skaiaa noted full-thickness frostbite on his fingers and advised him of the seriousness and possibility of amputation. All help was declined. Kristina Marjanovic went solo to the summit on the 29th, leaving Mlinaric in camp by himself. On June 30th, Mlinaric again declined assistance in the morning. They said they would descend the ridge using their own resources. After attempting to break camp in excellent weather on the afternoon of June 30th, the team came to the NPS camp and requested help in getting down the mountain. The Park Service team consisting of Ranger Kevin Wright, volunteers Nick Armitage, Weston Morrison, Roanna Wick and Sven Skaiaa, made a plan to leave the next morning if conditions were favorable. On the morning of July 1st, Dr. Skaiaa dressed the patient's fingers and prepared him for the descent. The Park Service team short-roped Mlinaric down the ridge from 17,200 feet and lowered him down the fixed lines, reaching 14,200-foot camp in the afternoon. He was re-evaluated by Park VIP and paramedic Rocco Pergola. On the morning of July 2nd, the Park Service Lama helicopter transported Mlinaric to basecamp where he was transferred to an air taxi and then taken to Alaska Regional Hospital in Anchorage.

**Analysis**

The initial frostbite was caused from removing gloves during very cold and windy conditions. This is one of the most common causes of severe frostbite on Denali. Most patients report being surprised at the speed of onset and resulting severity of their injuries. Mlinaric's injury may have worsened due to remaining at high camp rather than descending during the first available opportunity. He denies that any refreezing occurred during that time; however, the delay in seeking medical treatment could affect the degree of permanent damage to his hands. (Source: Kevin Wright, Ranger, Denali National Park)

## SUDDEN DEATH ON SUMMIT
### Alaska, Mount McKinley, West Buttress

This Alpine Ascents International climbing expedition flew into the base camp of Mount McKinley on June 20th with two guides and six clients, one of whom was James P. Nasti (51), a first time client of that company. The two guides were Michael Horst (lead guide) and Suzanne Allen (assistant guide). The expedition departed base camp early in the morning of June 22nd and arrived at the 14,200-foot camp on the evening of June 28th. The trip to 14,200 feet was uneventful with the exception that one client was sent back, at his request, to base camp on June 25th. The expedition conducted one carry of food and gear on July 1st to acclimatize, then moved to the

17,200-foot camp on July 2nd. The group rested at high camp on July 3rd and planned their summit attempt for the following day. Horst stated that the summit day temperature at high camp was estimated at 10 to 15 degrees Fahrenheit and with light winds.

Following breakfast and hot drinks the two rope teams departed at 1050, arriving at Denali Pass at 1200. From there the teams climbed one hour at a time, taking a 15-minute break between each stretch. The guides stated they evaluated each climber's physical and mental condition every hour. The entire group was thought to be doing well. After arriving at the Football Field (19,600 feet) and resting they began their climb to the summit at 1800 and arrived there at 1905. The clients did not have packs on at this time since they had cached them on the Football Field and, at the direction of the guides, had put on additional layers of insulated clothing for the summit attempt itself. One of the clients, Mark Novak, who was a close personal friend of Nasti, stated that he thought most people, to include himself and Nasti, were overheating from the exertion and clothing layers, but neither he nor Nasti made any attempt to ventilate. Novak also stated that the ridge itself was windy, with a corresponding drop in temperature, but maintained that they both were still overheated when the incident occurred.

The expedition was traveling as two rope teams: the first, being lead by Horst, reached the summit at 1905. The second rope, being lead by Allen, was estimated to be ten minutes behind. Just below the summit of Denali there is a small flat bowl approximately 20 feet in diameter, and after reaching this point Horst began retrieving the rope and bringing in his clients. The clients were arrayed on the rope behind Horst as follows: Sean Carver, James Nasti, and Mark Novak. Carver reached the location where Horst was, and as Horst continued bringing in the rope, it went tight. Horst continued to give encouragement to the remaining two climbers but did not get any response from Nasti. He could only see Novak and after asking him what was going on, Novak said, "Jim is on his back and unresponsive." Novak later attested that Nasti was right at the edge of the bowl when he slipped down vertically approximately three feet from the track. Nasti began plunging his ice ax and kicking his crampons into the slope in an attempt to regain the track when he suddenly slumped forward onto the head of the ax, rolled over onto his right side and then to his back, and then slid down about two feet. He remained face up with his head pointed downhill. It was at this time that Horst asked Novak what was going on. Novak was the only person who witnessed this event. The other rope team was still out of sight and the other two climbers, Horst and Carver, were out of visual sight of Nasti.

Horst immediately moved down to where Nasti was and upon arrival, found Nasti "completely unresponsive and not breathing". He further stated that Nasti did not have a pulse but did have an open airway. Horst administered two rescue breaths and checked for response to verbal and painful stimulation. Nasti was still unresponsive so Horst began cardio pulmonary resuscitation. After a few cycles of CPR, Carver appeared, stated that he was an EMT, and took over rescue breathing while Horst continued compressions at a 15:2 ratio. After 15 minutes of CPR, Allen arrived and took over compressions; Horst in-turn radioed the National Park Service (NPS) patrol at the 14,200-foot camp and reported the situation. The mountaineering ranger at that camp (Kevin Wright) advised that they continue CPR while the physician volunteering with the patrol, Dr. Sven Skaiaa, was consulted. Within about four minutes, Wright radioed back and instructed them to continue CPR for an additional ten minutes. After the ten minutes had elapsed, Nasti was still unresponsive to verbal and painful stimuli, did not have a carotid pulse, and his pupils were fixed and dilated. The NPS ranger then advised Horst to discontinue CPR and to take care of his remaining clients.

The winds were increasing on the summit and after standing still for over a half hour it was imperative that the team descend. Further instructions were given to move the deceased away from the track and to cover and mark the body. Nasti's body was secured with his ice ax and a snow picket and the expedition returned to the 17,200-foot camp uneventfully.

Based on the location of the deceased, it was determined by the NPS that any retrieval attempts would require an expedition of at least six individuals solely dedicated for that purpose. To arrive at a point along the summit ridge that would allow a safe lower to the Football Field would require a 500-foot traverse along a steeply angled knife ridge. From there, multiple lowers would be required to reach the 17,200-foot camp. No such team was available on the mountain so the decision was made to postpone any retrieval attempt until the following year. At that time the situation would be readdressed as to its feasibility. Two additional Alpine Ascents International expeditions were at the 17,200-foot camp and were asked that if the possibility arose, to attempt a burial of the deceased, thus removing him from sight of other climbers or flight seeing aircraft. The leader of this attempt, guide Willi Prittie, departed the 17,200-foot camp on July 6th, accompanied by fellow guides Alex Everett, John Prudhomme, David Kratsch, Ian Wolfe plus their respective clients. These two expeditions attained the summit just prior to 1700, and after spending an hour and a half digging, buried James Nasti approximately two feet below the surface of the snow.

## Analysis

Without an autopsy, the cause of death will never be known, but it should be noted that, according to family members and the medical information James Nasti submitted to Alpine Ascents International, he did not have any known pre-existing medical condition or medical history that could have caused his sudden death. Nasti was also physically fit for the endeavor and had supplemented his normal weekly fitness routine with a specific six-month training program to prepare for the climb. After a careful expedition review, the NPS could not find any contributing factors to the incident. Furthermore, the NPS found that the guides' decision-making process and leadership was sound and consistent with accepted safe guiding practices. Through no apparent fault of anyone, this was a tragic ending to an otherwise a successful climbing expedition. (Source: John A. Loomis, Ranger, Denali National Park)

## SUDDEN DEATH — NEAR DENALI PASS
### Alaska, Mount McKinley, West Buttress

At 2200 on July 7, Ranger John Loomis received a call on the emergency call out phone from ranger Kevin Wright at the 14,200-foot camp. Wright reported that he had received FRS radio transmissions from Peter Anderson (Rainier Mountaineering Guide) at 17,200 feet about a fatality on the Mountain Trip group while descending. Loomis contacted Helicopter Manager Dave Kreutzer and Ranger Joe Reichert and all met at the ranger station.

At 2304 we received a direct satellite phone call from Constantine (Con) Severis at high camp on the West Buttress. Severis confirmed that Pungkas Tri Baruno (20) had died near the rocks at the bottom of the traverse from Denali Pass (approximately 17,400 feet). At the time of this phone call, Severis had just returned to camp, so the rangers encouraged him to get food and water and call back at 2330. With the name of the deceased confirmed, Loomis began the public relations process of notifying the family. Unable to reach a person at the Indonesian consulate, he phoned the American embassy in Indonesia and was able to relay the information to them so that they could make arrangements to make the notification.

Severis contacted the ranger Search and Rescue room again at 2337. Rangers were able to learn that the team had reached the summit about 1600 that day. They had departed high camp at 0900 and it had been a smooth day until just before the incident. Pungkas was traveling slowly on the descent, reported Severis, but no slower than other tired clients whom he had worked with. The time of the incident was around 2000. Severis attempted to resuscitate Pungkas for 30-45 minutes where he had collapsed. With additional help from guides, Josh Kling (the second Mountain Trip guide) and Greg Vernovage (Alaska Mountaineering School) who had arrived from the high camp, they attempted to transport Pungkas back to camp, but due to the deep snow, lack of a sled, and fatigue they were forced to leave him.

During this phone call Severis reported that Hartman Nugraha (the second client on the team) was especially distraught. The rangers encouraged the guides to not let Nugraha spend the night alone. Josh Kling said he would be able to move into the Indonesians' tent. The rangers encouraged him to take care of his group and call again in the morning. A check-in time was set for 1000. During this time Bill Allen of Mountain Trip, had been alerted and was making plans to come to Talkeetna in the morning with a friend of the group to translate for Nugraha. At 0405 on July 8, ranger Loomis received a call from the family in Indonesia and answered basic questions asked of him by a brother of the deceased.

Wright and Nick Armitage moved Pungkas to the 17,200-foot camp on July 9. On July 10 Bill Billmeier and Jacob Schmitz, guides for Mountain Trip, assisted the NPS by clipping Pungkas into the short haul rope under the Lama helicopter. These guides were at high camp on their own expedition and having them perform the hook-up allowed ranger Wright to descend and prepare more of the 14,200-foot camp to be removed.

## Analysis

Through interviewing the three survivors on this expedition, it appears that all regular safety measures were followed on this particular summit climb. Once Pungkas collapsed, Severis made every effort possible to resuscitate him using all appropriate wilderness emergency medical protocols. Following my investigation it appears that this was a natural, albeit surprising, fatality. By every report, guides Severis and Kling progressed up the route at a pace that was normal for climbers who have not experienced high altitude before. Hartman Nugraha confirmed that communication with the guides was clear and that they understood the challenges of the climb each day.

Based on Nugraha's statement, the language barrier between the guides and the clients did not inhibit communication to the point that it was detrimental to understanding daily operations. Perhaps the guides were not able to read the subtleties in behavior change that may have been more apparent if they shared a common language and culture. More likely it appears that common warning signs that happen to climbers at altitude were not present. The nausea experienced by each client was known by the guides and recuperation time was allowed for before the group climbed higher. Headaches, ataxia, and loss of appetite were not present in this group.

The autopsy report from the State Medical Examiner's office states that the cause of death was "Sudden Arrhythmic Cardiac Death". (Source: Joe Reichert, Ranger, Denali National Park)

*(Editor's Note: Two sudden deaths within days of each other would have to be considered highly unusual and unique. No other incidents like this have occurred on Mount McKinley.)*

## FALL ON ROCK, FATIGUED, PLACED NO PROTECTION, "TOO RELAXED"
### Arizona, Cochise Stronghold

Ever since my fall I have been reliving the events of that day, but I have also been psychoanalyzing why I fell. I can still vividly see the fall. I have also pondered, for weeks now, whether or not I should post my "accident". You see, for me the only justification for bringing this to light is the hope that someone—anyone—could benefit from my predicament and, hopefully, learn from it to reduce the possibility of a similar accident happening to them.

I was climbing in Cochise with a good friend the other week. Things were pretty much typical except, maybe, for the fact that I was running on little sleep and that I was in a negative mood. I tied in as usual and made my typical pre-climb assessments. I was confident enough, the grade was well within my ability; I was "up" for the climb. But, something was wrong. Something must have been wrong because I fell. Upon reflection I can clearly see that I was too relaxed. I was too mellow for the seriousness of the climb and, perhaps more specifically, the seriousness of the landing.

I led up maybe 15 feet feeling comfortable. I had not placed any gear. At one point I do remember looking at a placement, but decided not to put anything in because I was thinking I had to save the gear to finish the pitch. At one moment I stopped. At that moment I recall thinking, hey, I have no secure handholds and poor foot placements. I then recall thinking that I should put in a piece. But, in the split seconds that followed my right foot skated and the next thing I realized was that something was wrong; I was falling. I somehow turned myself around, sliding down the face with my palms on the very steep (near vertical) slab, my feet leading. In the next instant I was on the ground and my left foot was jammed into a crevice. The sole of my foot was up, my heal was extended down (I hyper extended my ankle; dorsi-flection), my predicament only then coming to realization.

I have only one question for myself. That is, why had I stopped in (or perhaps more correctly, moved into) a place with no handholds and only marginal foot placements? Especially given that I had no gear in. This question haunts me a bit, because it makes no sense to me. Being comfortable on a route is not new to me, although I think that I may have been a bit too relaxed in this case. I can usually mange to increase my excitation level to a point consistent with my assessed level of the risk of the climb. Perhaps, in this case, I failed to do that.

I have a slight brake in my Talus, and the doc said that I would heal with little to no long-term problems. But, I want to learn from this experience and, yet, I am not yet quite sure what it is that I need to learn.

As a side note, I have witnesses multiple falls from climbers. In one case a friend zipped three pieces and landed at my feet, on his back, on top of the rope bag. To me the fall happened nearly instantaneously; it was over

(I thought) in a split second. Yet, for my fall, I can see all the events happening; I see myself sliding down, conscious of the fact that my palms were pressing against the rock, my feet in front of me, my knees slightly bent, and then the landing. I would surmise that it took less than 1 second, but I visualize it as a sequence of clear events with time to ponder and think about the event. (Source: David Arthur Sampson)

## STRANDED – INABILITY TO REMOVE ANATOMICAL PROTECTION
### California, Yosemite Valley, Bishops Terrace

On April 12, Tim Barthel (51), Jon Becker (50), Brant Herrett (55), and I, Steve Latif (46), decided to climb Bishops Terrace, a one-pitch 5.8 at the Church Bowl. At 1600 I started leading with Brant belaying. This was my first time on the route and about 80 feet up the pitch I found myself at a wide crack headed a bit to the right. It looked like the easiest option, so, thinking it was the standard line, I placed a cam and continued up.

A short way past my protection I realized I was in the off-width variation shown on the topo, not where I wanted be. The crack wasn't particularly hard and I'm comfortable leading most 5.10, but I'm not that experienced with wide cracks. Furthermore, I was already five to ten feet over my last piece and I didn't have any large pro for the next 15–20 feet. I was definitely outside my comfort zone, so I began backing down to the main crack.

My left leg was in the off-width and my right foot on the face. I moved down two or three feet and found that my left knee was getting stuck. Below me the crack constricted slightly, and the more I tried to free myself by pushing and pulling any way I could, the more stuck I became. After about five minutes of this, I was worn out and called down to my friends for help.

While Brant kept me on belay with my lead rope, Tim belayed Jon as he led up the normal route. When Jon was sufficiently above me, he rigged an overhead directional for his lead rope, allowing Tim to hold him in place. He had brought up another rope, the end of which he dropped to me. He clipped it to my harness and he belayed me off his harness, providing the security of a top-rope while I struggled. That didn't help much, so he rigged another directional, clipped my top-rope through it, and tried to provide me some lift by pulling down on his side of the directional with his bodyweight. With the friction in the directional carabiner and the fact that I outweighed Jon, that effort was doomed as well. We even lubricated my knee with water and Jon got under me and pushed up on my foot and my knee. Nothing worked. The knee stayed jammed and it was starting to hurt, and after 20 minutes of pulling and pushing, we were both tired. It was pretty clear I wasn't going anywhere.

Being April and almost 1900, it was going to get dark and cold, so I yelled down to Tim that we should call for help. He notified the NPS by cell phone and in a few minutes several NPS team members showed up. Jeff, one of the rangers, led up and established an independent anchor just above me. He ran a static line through a pulley at that anchor and down to me and the team on the ground set up a 3:1 mechanical advantage system with pulleys. This time, when they pulled, I moved. My leg stretched and hurt like hell. It was incredibly painful, as though they were going to rip it off and I'd yell at them to stop. But with each pull, my leg worked its way out maybe a quarter or half an inch. They did that three times and then it just popped out. Pulling up on my foot instead of from my harness would only have forced the foot against my thigh, so it was necessary to pull as they did. Tim said later, "The rescue team had three guys pulling on a 3:1 and I was staring at that going, 'Holy Smokes!' I was cringing."

The team lowered me and then Jon to the ground. Jeff finished the pitch and rappelled from the regular anchors at the top. My knee was a little sore and sported a bruise, but I was able to walk on it. It was about 2030 by then, completely dark, and I was just beginning to get a little chilly. (Source: Steve Latif)

**Analysis**

Steve's was the first of two stuck knees the park team dealt with in 2008. In the second case, the climber was competent for the terrain and on the correct route and the climbing was fairly easy, but she became solidly jammed. It looked quite grim, even with a haul system, until we liberally applied a bottle of liquid dish soap to her leg. (Yes, we cleaned up our mess.) Extrapolating from these cases, we can assume a few self-rescued knees every year as well.

No harm was done here. Church Bowl is only 100 meters from the parking lot, but the risk increases if you're immobilized with nasty weather moving in and/or inadequate clothing and only your partner to help, such as being high on Middle Cathedral Rock or Matterhorn Peak.

Prevention: Entrapment can happen to anyone, so keep the possibility in mind on every wide move.

Self-rescue: Steve said that having the right protection on his rack would have enabled him to set his own anchor and pull himself out, but you can't count on a perfect location and Steve could not have counter-weighted himself. Jon was smart to set up an upper belay for Steve in case he did pop free, but since Steve's belay was off Jon's harness rather than independently anchored, Tim might have found himself trying to hold two big guys at once. Being able to set up efficient haul systems is critical, whether a simple 1:1 directional applying body-weight force or more complicated mechanical-advantage arrangements. Pulleys are incredibly more effective than carabiners. A small, high-quality, rescue-grade pulley is recommended for every climber's rack (not just one per party). Two pulleys in a party will build a 4:1 system for self-rescue of more serious injuries as well as for stuck knees.

Warning: This is not an instructional text. We have skipped several important details covered by self-rescue manuals. Understand your systems and apply force cautiously. (Source: John Dill, NPS Ranger, Yosemite National Park)

## STRANDED – YOGI-PHOBIA, UNFAMILIAR WITH EQUIPMENT
### California, Yosemite, Half Dome

Janet (32) spent May 9 hanging out at the base of Half Dome while her friends made an ascent of the Regular NW Face route. They had camped there the night before and had suspended their food from a tree to keep it from animals. At mid-day a bear wandered into camp and began sniffing the food. Concerned about becoming lunch herself, Janet jumared up an old fixed line to the top of the first pitch.

Eventually the bear left, but when Janet tried to descend, she found that 30 feet of snow piled on the bottom of the rope over the winter had stretched the line too tight to attach her rappel device. Her friends were high on the face, not in position to help, and she was marginally dressed for a spring night on the wall at 7,000 feet. At 1730 Janet called the NPS.

Three SAR team members climbed the slab approach from Mirror Lake to the base of the wall, arriving at dusk. One ascended the fixed line, and then he and Janet rappelled on NPS ropes. They all descended the slabs to the Valley, including Janet, who had seen one bear too many.

### Analysis

Janet was a climber, but she may have lacked the experience to realize that she could jumar down the fixed line as well as up. Her party also may not have understood that hanging food in a tree is no longer permitted in the park. Bear canisters are required in Wilderness areas, although they aren't necessary on a climbing route if the food is well beyond reach of Yogi. But watch out for ground squirrels (they free-solo 5.11) and ravens. Food storage requirements, other wilderness regulations, and Leave No Trace practices are all explained to climbers when they get their wilderness permit, which is required for camping at the base of Half Dome. (Source: John Dill, NPS Ranger, Yosemite National Park)

## FALL ON ROCK, INADEQUATE PROTECTION, POOR COMMUNICATION, INADEQUATE MEDICAL TRAINING
### California, Yosemite Valley, El Capitan

At 0330 on May 15, Matt Christensen (26) and Tony McClane (20) climbed fixed lines to Sickle Ledge on El Capitan and started up pitch 5 of the Nose (31 pitches, VI 5.9 C1 per SuperTopo). They traveled light, with one 60-m rope, hoping to summit that night. The climb went smoothly and they were happy with their progress. After completing pitch 24, Tony belayed just below Camp V, at the spot marked "OK bivy for 1" on SuperTopo. It was now about 2030, a little after dark.

Matt led pitch 25. To avoid rope drag, he placed no protection on the easier section up to the ledge just above Camp V (marked "OK bivy for 2" on the topo). Then he continued up a thin aid crack toward the Glowering Spot. Tony could not see Matt by this time because of darkness and the shape of the wall. After the rope had paid out for a while Matt seemed to slow or stop for a few minutes. Then Tony heard, "Oh shit! Oh shit!" and the sounds of falling. Just as Matt hit the ledge, Tony felt tension come on the rope, which he thinks cushioned the impact.

Tony started shouting Matt's name and became alarmed when he got no answer, so he anchored the rope and jugged up it using Matt's body as a counter-weight. When he reached the ledge, about five minutes after the fall, Matt was just lying there. The ledge sloped and Matt was head down, so Tony helped him sit up. His eyes were open and he seemed conscious, but when Tony asked, "Are you OK? What's my name?" Matt didn't say anything. He didn't seem to know what had happened, and Tony thought maybe he couldn't hear. He wasn't fighting, but he resembled a drunk person—moving, but not purposefully or effectively.

Despite his helmet, Matt had a laceration on the back of his head and patches of blood the size of a dinner plate were scattered everywhere, maybe half a liter altogether. When Tony saw all the blood, he thought Matt might die. They had left Matt's cell phone in camp, so Tony started signaling for help by flashing his light down toward the Valley.

A Polish team of two was at Camp VI, two pitches higher, so Tony shouted up to them but got no response. Someone on the ground heard him, however, and contacted the NPS by cell phone at 2100. About 30 minutes later, park rangers in El Cap Meadow broadcast toward the cliff with a loudspeaker, "If you need a rescue flash your light." Tony answered with a flash. The rangers replied, "To answer 'Yes', flash three times, to answer 'No' flash once," and then they began asking "Yes/No" questions. The night was calm and clear—excellent conditions for communicating with parties on the wall. Tony was gradually able to describe the situation.

When asked, Tony signaled that he had no medical training. The rangers took that into account in guiding him through a medical exam, which extracted more information: The patient had suffered a head laceration with heavy bleeding and a loss of consciousness of two to five minutes. He currently had no trouble breathing, no uncontrolled bleeding, had a pulse at the wrist, no apparent chest injury, no bones visible, normal feeling and movement in hands and feet, and was seated on a ledge.

When communicating like this, however, misunderstandings always occur. In this case, when determining which member of the party was answering the questions, the rangers came to believe they were talking directly with the injured climber himself. Since Tony had been excellent at responding clearly, they had the impression the patient was fully alert and oriented, when, in fact, Matt was curled into a ball, making no sense, and hardly able to respond to Tony, let alone to a loudspeaker a half mile away in the dark.

Tony wanted immediate assistance. The rangers agreed but told him that they would not be able to reach him until after daybreak. After advising Matt to try to not move his head because of the risk of a neck injury, they left to prepare the team, still with the impression that he was fully alert.

Though not a great bivy, the ledge was ample for both of them to sit, and Tony had been able to build a secure anchor for the night. They had enough water, but having packed for a speed ascent, they had very little clothing, and the night was chilly. Per the rangers' instructions, Tony huddled next to Matt to keep him as quiet and still as possible.

Despite Tony's efforts, Matt became more active over time, playing with the anchor, and saying, "Tony, we've got to go down," and, "You're on belay." As dawn was breaking, Matt got up, and Tony thought he was just taking a pee over the side. He asked Matt what he was doing and Matt replied, "I'm going to bed". It turned out he wanted to go down to Camp V where there was a better bivy. By the time Tony realized what he was up to, Matt had untied and was out of reach, 10-15 feet down on another ledge. Then he took off his harness and down-climbed a 5.7 crack all the way to Camp V. Tony shouted down, "What the #&%!! are you doing? Put on your harness!" Matt scrambled back up the crack and put on his harness.

Matt wasn't completely alert but he was now looking Tony in the eye without getting distracted and was answering simple questions. Tony thought that Matt would have known by now if he were hurt. His apparently improved mental and physical condition—evidenced by his downclimb—convinced Tony that Matt could probably safely move around and even jumar, so maybe he didn't need a rescue. He asked Matt, "Do you want to jumar or do you want a rescue?" Matt replied, "Jumar."

The NPS "spotters" were back shortly after dawn with the loudspeaker and a telescope. For the first time they were able to see exactly where Matt and Tony were. They asked, "Wave your arms if you need a rescue." Tony did not answer, thinking Matt would be able to make it to the summit. He decided to finish leading Matt's pitch to the Glowering Spot and then see if Matt could competently jumar. If Matt made decent time, Tony reasoned, he'd be capable of summiting. Otherwise they would ask for a rescue.

About 0700, as Tony was leading the pitch, the NPS helicopter hovered nearby and asked, via loudspeaker, if they wanted a rescue. Tony waved them off. Tony recalls, "Matt was down at our bivy ledge. He had me on a Grigri so I wasn't concerned that he was belaying competently, and if I asked for rope he responded right away. The helicopter left and it seemed like the NPS got the message. I made it to the anchor and Matt jugged in a reasonable amount of time. When he got up to me, he was rigged correctly for jugging. I asked, 'Can you do this? Are you OK?' and he said he thought he was capable."

The spotters stayed in the meadow all day to monitor the party's progress, and two other rescuers hiked to the summit to communicate directly with Tony and Matt as they neared the top.

The Polish team tossed a fixed line down from Camp VI, enabling Tony and Matt to join them. From that point on, the Poles climbed ahead and fixed Tony's rope at each pitch. Now Tony could let Matt jumar first to be sure he rigged and climbed correctly. He was comfortable that Matt was performing well on the wall but was fairly sure that he wouldn't be able to hike out on his own.

Tony recalled, "I asked him how he was feeling and he said, 'Better'. He didn't seem to be getting worse; otherwise I wouldn't have wanted him to jug. But he wasn't bright and cheery and sometimes he would go to sleep at the anchors and I would wake him when he was ready to go.

"I never tried to initiate a rescue during the climb out, but at one point, above Camp VI, Matt started jugging and wasn't doing very well and said, 'I'm done for the day'. He came back to the anchor, rested 10-15 minutes, and then jumared it decently. During that interval I thought he wasn't capable of getting out on his own and I was pissed that I hadn't asked for help first thing that morning. But he was effective, even on the overhanging sections, and I doubt the spotters in the meadow would have noticed any warning signs."

However, by the time the Poles topped out at 1530-1600, they and Tony felt that Matt was deteriorating, so the rescuers at the summit radioed for reinforcements to be flown up. When Matt reached the top, he collapsed in exhaustion. He was met by a medical team that found him oriented to person, place, time, and events, but his responses were sluggish, occasionally confused, and he was having trouble staying awake. He also complained of pain and tenderness in his neck at the C-6 and C-7 vertebrae. He was immobilized, packaged in a litter, and short-hauled with a ranger-medic off the lip of El Cap to an EMS helicopter waiting in El Cap Meadow.

The final diagnosis was a subdural hematoma, a fractured skull, and the head laceration, but no serious injury to his neck. Matt spent several days under observation in the hospital ICU. He avoided surgery and has made a full recovery—except for a blank spot in his life. He said, "The last thing I remember of the climb was making the first few placements on that pitch. I woke up in the hospital four days later."

## Analysis

Experience: Matt said, "I thought we were doing phenomenally well, really efficient. We're not super-climbers by any means, but we have 3-5 years of intensive climbing experience, including several multi-pitch routes and fast ascents, and we work well as a team. We were moving at a reasonable pace, no arguments, and not being rushed or cutting corners."

Equipment: They did cut corners, however, by taking just one rope. This is common practice for fast ascents, but that does leave the party with little margin for self-rescue, e.g., to belay to an injured partner or make a quick retreat. It put Tony in the position of having to rely initially on brain-injured Matt to rig and ascend correctly, and then to rely on the Poles for help—a wise move but not a predictable option.

Tony said, "If we'd thought someone would get injured, we would definitely have taken more than one rope. We assumed we would not get hurt. We don't fall off 5.9 and shouldn't be falling off C1 either. We assumed wrong, but an accident seemed very unlikely. It was a surprise." Other common surprises include broken holds, rockfall, damaged/stuck rope, dropped gear, and significantly under-rated pitches.

The Fall: The free-climbing on that pitch is hard, so Matt was probably aiding. He was caught by protection about 25 feet above the ledge, but we don't know where the fall started or why. At least two failed pieces, possibly fixed, contributed to his striking the ledge. The take-home message is that falls can happen to anyone.

Getting to Matt: When Tony jugged the rope to reach Matt after the fall, both climbers were loading Matt's highest remaining piece. Tony didn't know the quality of the placement or whether it had been weakened by stopping the fall. He also did not know what remained to catch him if the top piece pulled, and in a hard fall, his ascenders could have damaged or severed his rope, but he'd never had to rescue someone before and didn't know what else to do. He figured that if the top piece had held Matt's fall, it should be good for jugging. It might have been better to self-belay up to Matt, and Tony had enough rope for the task. Several bivy and anchor bolts along the way offered protection and the climbing was fairly easy.

Communications: Playing "Twenty Questions" in the dark is fertile ground for misunderstandings. In this case it put Matt at risk in several ways. Had we realized the issues that night, we would have explained the situation to Tony or ignored his wave-off in the morning. Some advice: Carrying a cell phone or FRS radio can prevent such a problem. A phone must have service where you climb and it must have a battery fully charged for emergencies, not drained by calling your friends at every belay. You may need it for several calls with rescuers, not just a single 911 contact.

The NPS does not monitor FRS radios, so leave one with a reliable friend. Treat at least one set of radio batteries as emergency gear—no chit-chat. Unlike cell phones, FRS radios can talk directly to each other, but they do have range and terrain limitations.

Medical issues: Tony thought and acted reasonably, given his lack of emergency medical training, but he did not understand the risks that Matt faced. This is the most important lesson in this incident.

- A blow to the head resulting in Matt's altered behavior is likely to have caused bleeding inside the skull that presses on the brain. It may only become serious hours later and then prove fatal.
- A patient like Matt, though seemingly aware, is capable of semi-intelligent but potentially disastrous actions, as evidenced by Matt's incredible free-solo-in-the-dark down-climb. As he continued to the summit, Matt might have untied himself, mis-rigged his Jumars, or taken Tony off belay. Advice: If you have to leave a head-trauma patient to go for help, devise several secure tie-ins, restrain the arms if necessary, and confiscate knives and other articles that could cause harm.
- Anyone with Matt's mechanism of injury is at high risk for a broken neck. It can sometimes be ruled out if the patient is truly alert, but Matt did not qualify. Waiting quietly for a rescue and hoping Matt cooperated was medically safer than self-rescue.

Final Advice: A First Responder course, especially the Wilderness version, covers this material. No climber should be without this training. One trained person in the party is not enough, since he or she might be the patient.

Final Word: No one wants to be rescued, because of pride, self-reliance, or public perception. Tony left the decision up to Matt, but as he stated later, "When someone is that disoriented, their opinion doesn't really matter, does it?" He's right. The choice of self-rescue was not Matt's to make. (Source: Matt Christianson, Tony McClane, and John Dill, NPS Ranger, Yosemite National Park)

## FALL ON ROCK, HANDHOLD DISLODGED – FALL ON ROCK
### California, Sierra Nevada, Palisades Region

At 0700 on July 13, J.C. (47) and B.Y. (47) set out from camp at 10,000 feet at Brainard Lake on the South Fork of Big Pine Creek intending to climb the Northwest Ridge (5.7) on The Thumb. The previous day's weather included afternoon and evening thunderstorms. As the pair approached the peak, they repeatedly discussed the early appearance of clouds and whether they should consider turning back to camp. The weather improved around 0900 and as they reached the bottom of the northwest couloir, they decided to climb up and turn around if the weather deteriorated. Approximately 500 feet up the loose scree, talus, and snow of the couloir, the pair turned right to climb a third class wall to reach the start of the roped pitches. J.C. went left and B.Y. went right, with the plan to meet 100 feet higher. J.C. was 15 feet up on the wall when he pulled and dislodged a large block weighing at least 100 pounds. He could not prevent the rock from striking him and was knocked off his stance, subsequently falling backwards into the couloir with the block landing on top of his legs. He was wearing a small pack and helmet and did not hit his head. J.C. is a physician and was able to assess his injuries, which included deep lacerations of the left thigh, right shin, and left hand, a cracked front tooth, bruises to the left arm and ribcage, and a possible pneumothorax (collapsed lung). He was alert and had no obvious broken bones.

There were no other climbers in the area or cell phone reception. The pair had first aid gear and used ace bandages and duct tape to stabilize the bleeding from the lacerations. J.C. determined that he had no immediate life-threatening injuries. Despite pain and a possible pneumothorax, he decided they should attempt a self-rescue instead of B.Y. hiking out for help. They descended the couloir with two single rope 60 meter rappels, with J.C. rappelling and B.Y. down-climbing. J.C. took two prescription pain pills, and they hiked down 2000 feet and a few miles to camp in five hours with periods of rain and hail. J.C. was able to walk slowly without help using trekking poles. Upon reaching camp around 1700, J.C. was too exhausted to hike five more miles to the car. J.C. again assessed his injuries. He was no longer bleeding and was breathing comfortably at rest at 10,000 feet. He decided they should eat, hydrate, sleep, and hike out at first light. B.Y. agreed and they hiked out the next day with B.Y. carrying most of the gear. They arrived at the car three hours later and drove two hours to Mammoth Lakes emergency room, where J.C. was found to have a fractured left rib with a 40% collapse of the left lung. A chest tube was inserted with full re-inflation of the lung. The lacerations on his legs were irrigated and left open for later closure. J.C. was discharged four hours later and drove seven hours home that evening. He was back in the office seeing patients the following afternoon. Four weeks later, J.C. was fully recovered and climbing in Yosemite. (Source: J.C.)

*(Editor's Note: We thank Dr. J.C. for submitting this report. He was fortunate to be able to manage his own medical care, and it is commendable that he and B.Y. were able to self-rescue.)*

## FALL ON ROCK – MISJUDGED PENDULUM
### California, Yosemite Valley, El Capitan

At 0545 on July 18, Eric Ruderman (32) and Skiy DeTray (31) started a one-day ascent of the Nose on El Capitan (31 pitches, VI 5.9 C1, per SuperTopo). They were a strong team with several years of experience and over 20 walls between them and they climbed at a high standard. Typical of fast ascents, they carried one 60-m rope and they "short-fixed"; i.e., after reaching the end of a pitch, the leader pulled up any remaining slack, anchored the rope, and began rope-soloing the next pitch to save time. Meanwhile, the second jugged, and when he reached the anchor he started belaying the leader.

Skiy led the first block of pitches to the base of the Stove Legs. Eric led from there, reaching the top of Boot Flake (top of pitch 16) by 0900. They were on schedule, with no glitches so far. Skiy jugged up to Eric and took over the lead. Eric lowered him out on pitch 17 to attempt the King Swing, a long and tricky pendulum to the left. He made the swing on his first try and pulled himself over to Eagle Ledge.

Of several ways for Eric to follow the pendulum, they had decided that the fastest and most efficient was for Skiy to back-clean; i.e., to remove all his protection behind him as he climbed the remaining 70 feet from Eagle Ledge to the anchor at the top of 17. That way the rope would run free between the anchor at 16—the top of Boot Flake, where Eric waited—and the anchor at 17, giving Eric the highest pendulum point for following the swing. The two anchors are approximately 50 feet apart and at roughly the same level, although out of sight of each other.

Skiy needed rope to begin short-fixing pitch 18 while leaving enough for Eric to lower himself under control across the King Swing. He began pulling rope and yelled over to Eric, "Stop me while you still have enough for the lower out." Eric looked at his remaining rope and yelled back, "That should do it," so Skiy anchored the rope and began short-fixing pitch 18, with his Grigri on his harness as a self-belay.

They estimated that Skiy had pulled over 50 feet or more of slack, and since another 50 feet or so stretched back to pitch 16, Eric figured he still had about 100 feet piled at his feet for following the pendulum. He rigged his ascenders on the line and attached them to his harness. He pulled the rope back through them until the line to Skiy's anchor was tight. The radius of his pendulum was the distance from his ascenders to the anchor at 17, roughly 50 feet. He tied in short to his harness just underneath the ascenders to back them up and left the end of the rope also tied to his harness. The estimated 100 feet of slack rope lay between those two knots.

Eric looked at the distance he needed to go and at the pile of rope available. It looked like plenty, so he grabbed the mid-point of the slack and fed it through a carabiner at his anchor, resulting in a 50-foot bight—a length of doubled rope—on the other side of the carabiner from himself.

He began lowering himself down and across the gap by simply holding on to the doubled rope and feeding it back through the anchor carabiner hand-over-hand. After lowering about 25 feet, he ran out of rope, since half the bight had fed through to his side of the carabiner and he was now holding the end of the bight, which was still on the other side of the carabiner, in his hands. He knew that if he let go of it, he would swing left, uncontrolled except for friction on the rock and in his system. He looked at the potential swing. A corner blocked his view, but the arc seemed insignificant, so he dropped the rope.

As Skiy—already 15 to 20 feet up pitch 18—watched from above, Eric swung above and past Eagle Ledge and struck a corner farther left with his arm, head, and back. To Skiy the impact didn't seem hard, but Eric was immediately limp, hanging upside down and motionless.

Skiy's yells to Eric brought no response, so he down-climbed to the anchor and rappelled on his slack. Eric was hanging inverted, with the pack contorting him in an awkward position, and bleeding profusely from a laceration on the back of his head. Skiy asked, "Eric are you with me?" But Eric just mumbled. Skiy got the pack off and turned him upright. And at that point, a few minutes after the impact, Eric started to come around. His most prominent complaint was his left wrist—very painful and obviously broken or dislocated. Skiy decided there was not much he could do medically where they were. Despite, or maybe because of, the possibility of internal head and back injuries, moving him 20 feet down to Eagle Ledge seemed better than hanging on the wall.

Skiy rigged Eric's Grigri just below the ascenders, unclipped the backup knot, and had Eric stand in a sling to un-weight the rope so the ascenders could be removed. Each climber was now able to rappel with a Grigri on his own line, except that Eric had only one good hand. Skiy dropped down to Eagle Ledge and controlled the tension on Eric's rope so that Eric only had to operate the lever on his Grigri. The descent was painful, as his wrist hung unsupported. They reached the ledge about 15 minutes after the accident. (Luckily, Skiy had just enough rope left to reach Eagle Ledge without having to build an intermediate anchor.)

Once Eric got securely anchored on the ledge, Skiy stopped the bleeding with his shirt and performed a more thorough head-to-toe exam. Eric's wrist was the most painful injury, but his spine was tender to palpation at the lower border of his rib cage and eventually the pain became excruciating. His neck was not tender and he had normal feeling and movement in both hands and both feet. Skiy fashioned a wrist splint with a pack strap and clothing, which helped ease the pain.

They initially considered the possibility of rappelling the route, but Skiy (a paramedic) and Eric (an EMTB) both realized that the potential for brain and spinal injuries made that option medically unwise as well as physically very difficult and risky; Eric needed to get off the route ASAP.

Skiy had started yelling as soon as they were secure on the ledge, and within 45 minutes a ranger was talking to them by loudspeaker. Skiy was able to convey Eric's condition.

Flying conditions were excellent, so two rescuers were short-hauled directly to Eagle Ledge by helicopter. Eric was immobilized in a litter, short-hauled to El Cap Meadow, and then, three and a half hours after his accident, he was transferred to an air ambulance. At Memorial Medical Center in Modesto he was diagnosed with a fractured 7th rib, contused lungs, a fractured wrist, one broken tooth, and the scalp laceration, but no serious head injury (probably thanks to his helmet). A few months of physical therapy led to a full recovery except for his memory. After letting go of his lower-out rope, the next thing he remembers is bleeding all over Skiy while hanging from his ascenders.

## Analysis

In May a very experienced and skilled climber was trying to free climb across the pendulum to Hollow Flake on the Salathé Wall after the leader had made the swing. He had no back-rope, thinking he was low enough and the radius long enough that if he fell he would not build up much speed. He was luckier than Eric, fracturing only his fibula when he struck Hollow Flake.

Why are swinging falls so dangerous? First, if you fall from, say, ten feet to one side of and level with your pivot point, you will have the same speed at the lowest point of your swing as you will falling straight down ten feet, except that you are moving sideways. Second, instead of landing on your feet, with "only" a broken leg, you're apt to strike an obstacle sideways, with high risk of life-threatening injuries to your head, neck, chest, and pelvis. If you're lucky you'll be able to extend (and sacrifice) an arm or a leg to absorb the blow, but don't bet on it because you may be spinning out of control. This is a severe example, but significant risk remains even if you've already lowered partway, as Eric discovered.

Why is the danger misjudged? In addition to not realizing the physics involved, maybe it's because we're born with a fear of heights, so a ledge ten feet below us seems farther away and more dangerous than a corner ten feet to the side. Maybe looking across the swing just doesn't produce the same shivers as looking down. This effect is not confined to neophytes, as the case at hand illustrates.

Prevention: Maximize the rope available to the follower. Eric could have extended his rope by untying the end from his harness (while staying tied in short) and passing the single strand, instead of the bight, through the lower-out carabiner. Skiy also suggests not short-fixing that pitch at al—at the cost of only a few minutes—to give all the rope to the second. A third option is a second rope, which has many other uses in an emergency, including the ability to descend El Cap routes anchor-to-anchor.

Eric said, "We were shooting for a one-day ascent, but my decision wasn't due to haste, and I definitely wanted to be safe. The distance across seemed short, and I thought I had enough rope to just put the bight through the let-out biner. I never even thought about untying the end from my harness for more distance. Even when I ran out of rope partway across, I consciously estimated the swing would only be 10-20 feet. When I let go I was confident and I remember thinking, 'I can run this out'. I just made a mistake in judging the swing."

Finally, Skiy made this medical observation: "I learned that I don't want to position myself below a heavily bleeding patient!" (Source: Eric Ruderman, Skiy DeTray, and John Dill, NPS Ranger, Yosemite National Park)

## FALL ON ROCK, PROTECTION PULLED OUT, NO HELMET
### California, Yosemite Valley, Church Bowl

On August 31, Tomoki Shibata (22) led Church Bowl Tree, a 5.10b crack, belayed by Hiroki Kishi. Shibata left his helmet at the base of the climb because the route was only one pitch long. From the ground up, in this order, he placed a camming device, another cam, a stopper, and a third cam. The stopper dislodged as he was climbing.

Details are sketchy, but when the stopper fell out, Shibata apparently realized that a single piece stood between him and the ground, and we think he decided to go for the bolt anchor several feet above. His feet were about 40 feet above the ground when his left hand-jam slipped out and he fell. His top piece pulled out under the force of the fall; he hit the ground on his feet and then tumbled over. The rope came tight just as he hit, absorbing some of the energy of the fall.

Shibata was carried 100 yards to the ambulance, examined at the Yosemite Medical Clinic, and released after treatment for a head laceration, a fractured right wrist, and a fractured left thumb.

### Analysis

Shibata had four years climbing experience, mostly on bolted face climbs up to 5.11a. He had been climbing cracks and traditional routes (placing protection on the lead) for about six months prior to the accident. Church Bowl Tree, a popular, accessible, and relatively difficult climb, is fairly easy to protect, yet it has been the scene of various miscalculations and ground falls. Belayers should watch for these situations on any climb and not be afraid to encourage inexperienced leaders to protect conservatively. If not sure of a placement, double it up. (Source: Aaron Smith and John Dill, NPS Rangers, Yosemite National Park)

## FALL ON ROCK, PROTECTION PULLED OUT
### California, Idyllwild, Suicide Rock

On September 5, Trevor Mathews (21), suffered significant head trauma and remains in intensive care. His friend and climbing partner, Claire McKay (22), was treated and released but will undergo facial reconstruction surgery to treat a fractured cheekbone. She also broke her arm and has severe bruising, some caused by being pelted with hail as she lay unconscious on a ledge.

In accounts after the accident, relatives, rescue workers, and fellow climbers say Mathews and McKay began their climb Saturday under near-perfect conditions and clear skies. They took the Captain Hook route up the cliff, which, despite its name, is regarded as a relatively safe and easy climb. Both are said to be experienced climbers who train at an indoor facility. Both were wearing helmets. They were on the second phase of their climb when Mathews, who was about 40 feet above McKay, slipped while trying to set a wedging device for his rope, according to McKay's father. A second device securing the rope to the rock pulled loose and Mathews fell. McKay was on the same rope and was slammed into the face of the rock and knocked unconscious when the rope pulled taut as Mathews plummeted.

Phil Sanchez and his climbing partner Richard Magner and other climbers scrambled to help. They called 911 and secured Mathews in a stretcher that was on-site, with Magner taking off his shirt and using it to pad Mathews' head. They were carrying him out to the road when Idyllwild and Riverside County firefighters arrived. He was taken by helicopter to Riverside County Regional Medical Center.

As rescuers turned their attention to McKay, the sky began to darken. Sanchez and Magner decided they would climb the cliff face to get to her. As they made their ascent, the rain and hail began, first the size of BB's but soon growing to the size of grapes. Magner, who remained shirtless, was being cut by the hail. Rescue workers planned to use a helicopter to lift McKay off the cliff but had to abort the mission when the storm blew in, Idyllwild Fire Department Capt. Alan Lott said, "We were notified by the pilot of the helicopter that he could no longer see the nose of his ship."

Sanchez and Magner climbed to an anchor point about 25 feet above McKay, set their rope and then rappelled down to her. By that time she was conscious and responsive. Sanchez then rappelled to the bottom and secured the rope so that McKay, despite her injuries, could rappel herself down, with Magner following. "I was capable and fully confident to help her out, so I was going to do it," Sanchez said. "It wasn't even a question of what the weather was like. It was, 'Someone's in trouble and I'm going to do everything in my power to help this person out.'" Getting to McKay took about half an hour, in Sanchez's estimation, and getting her down took about 45 minutes. Once she reached the bottom, rescue workers put her in a stretcher, splinted her injuries, and carried her out to the road so she could eventually be taken by helicopter to the hospital.

"The weather was so bad you couldn't even look up to see if they were rappelling with her because of the ice coming down and the rocks and debris coming down," said Capt. Tim Bingham of the Riverside County Fire Department. (Source: Edited from an article by Christian Berthelsen in the *Los Angles Times*)

## LOST IN THE DARK
### California, Yosemite, Half Dome

In late September, Aloysius "Apple" Leap (25) and I (Chris Tomasetti, 23) made our first trip to Yosemite for a week and a half of climbing. We'd been climbing pretty intensively for 3-4 years at a good standard, though no big walls. We had the idea we were going to do the Nose and the Regular Northwest Face of Half Dome on this trip. First we tried El Cap, sharing bivies and some gear with two other friends climbing as a separate party. When they decided to retreat, we forgot to have them leave the community poop tube behind. The next morning we rummaged through our haul bag looking for a substitute, but when we couldn't find anything, we reluctantly bailed, too, and set our sights on Half Dome.

We planned to hike up Thursday afternoon, October 2, sleep at the base, and allow two full days on the wall with a bivy on Big Sandy Ledge along the way. That would give us time to work the hard pitches and free the whole thing, but at noon on Thursday we discovered that the weather forecast had changed. It now called for a storm to hit at midnight Friday, which would catch us on Big Sandy. We had a quick conversation: We were leaving the park Sunday, so this was it: We either do Half Dome in a day and risk getting caught near the top by the storm, or we go home with nothing big to show for the trip, just some cragging. We decided to climb it in a day and not try to free it. We would do a little aiding through the bolt ladders and French free other moves as necessary. Starting at 0500 Friday would have us off by 1700-1800, we thought, or roughly 12 hours.

We took the slab route from Mirror Lake, got to the base of the wall around sunset, and were on the route by 0500 as planned. We left our sleeping bags and bivy sacks at the base. Underneath our climbing pants and shirts we wore synthetic tops and bottoms, and we stuffed fleece jackets, warm hats, rain jackets, and rain pants into our pack. We didn't bring mittens or gloves, but we did have helmets, headlamps, walkie-talkies (for windy pitches), Apples's cell phone with a good battery, and enough food and water for a day. We brought only one rope, a 70-m, but we had a big rack, figuring if the weather got bad we could rappel off, leaving gear behind.

We'd done our homework regarding the route, and the climbing went well—super smooth. We freed a lot of the pitches except for some of the cruxes. The rock was dry, but the clouds rolled in before sunset and I climbed the Zigzags in heavy fog, unable to see 30 feet. We finished at 2100, a total of 16 hours, a little behind schedule. Unfortunately the storm arrived earlier than we expected, and a mix of rain and snow began ten minutes after we topped out. We hadn't researched the descent; we only knew we had to go down the cables and then some steps—about 900 vertical feet of rock, in all—and that was it. We didn't know whether to go left, right, or straight ahead, or in what compass direction, and we didn't have a compass anyway. I think our mindset had been, 'It's just a hikers' trail, it can't be that bad.' It was dark and foggy, and despite our headlamps, we couldn't find anything.

We kept trying to follow little piles of rocks, thinking they were cairns marking the trail, but they weren't, and they took us in circles. It was really confusing. So we walked around for a couple of hours, trying to figure out what to do, and then it dawned on us that we had a cell phone. We weren't actually sure who we were going to call. We had buddies in Camp 4, but we didn't have their numbers, and we never thought to call 911. Finally we found in Apple's pocket an empty matchbook with the Yosemite Lodge number on the back.

We had a conversation with each other: "Should we call?" "Well, you can call, but I don't want to call." "Do we have any other choice, man?" "Well, you call, man, it's your phone." Calling for directions was not the thing we wanted to do, but it was either that or walk in circles all night, and we figured a hint or two would be all we needed.

The number on the matchbook was disconnected but it told us to dial a different number. I had Apple remember the last four digits and I remembered the first three. We dialed and told them what was going on and they connected me to Katie, the NPS dispatcher. I told her where we were and she asked if we had a compass or a GPS device. Of course we had neither, but at one point the fog lifted briefly and I could see the lights of the Valley, so I said, "If I'm looking at those lights, where should I go?" She replied, "Over your right shoulder, the cables are in that direction." We were totally turned around, absolutely lost. We couldn't even find where we had topped out. The time was about 2330.

We got off the phone, wandered around for another 15 minutes in the fog and rain, and sure enough, found the cables. They were slightly covered with ice by now and really cold on our bare hands. Upright stanchions held them off the ground as handrails, so we clipped our daisy chains to the cables with locking carabiners. That way a stanchion would stop us if we fell.

It took us a while but we eventually got down and found that the cables ended in a little saddle. We knew the cables led to steps but didn't know a saddle separated them, or how far apart they were—another surprise.

Once again we wandered around, couldn't find the steps, and had no idea where to go. So we called Katie back. "Where are these steps, we can't find them". She said, "If you're standing in the saddle with the cables to your back, you have to go up over the little hump and down and slightly to the left."

*(Ranger Dill notes: Chris and Apple were talking with the right person. Katie had spent three seasons patrolling the Half Dome trail and had seen just about everything.)*

Visibility was now down to 15-20 feet. It was still precipitating, a little heavier than a drizzle, but our rain gear was keeping us dry except for our hands. The wind was sporadic, at first none, then a strong gust forcing us to stop moving and turn our backs to it. We'd stay relatively warm if we kept moving, but it was pretty cold if we stopped. My backup plan was to walk in circles all night if we'd got stuck up there. It would have been a long night but we'd be OK.

We followed Katie's directions. We walked quite a ways and almost found the steps on our first try. We were looking at a tree that later turned out to be right next to the steps, but in the fog and rain and with only our head-lamps we thought, "This can't be the steps. If we walk down there, we'll be at the very edge and we'll fall off. Let's err on the side of caution and back off here." We couldn't tell if it just got gradually steeper or the world ended in a shear drop 20 feet ahead. We probably could have explored on belay but we didn't think of that. Maybe we were stuck in hiker mode.

So we talked to Katie again and she eventually transferred us to Kevin, the ranger who now had Katie's old job patrolling Half Dome. We got him out of bed in his camp a few miles down the trail and he was actually thinking of coming to get us, but we had just found three or four steps all by themselves in the middle of nowhere, and now Kevin had an idea of where we were. Over the phone he walked me down the slab another couple of hundred feet until we hit the final steps. By now it was about 0100.

We knew we could find the trail in the woods to get back to the bivy. We were kind of ashamed that we had to call and it would have been worse if Kevin had had to come for us. "You don't have to come out," I said. He asked us to call him when we got back to the bivy, but our cell phone had died by then. The clothing under our rain gear was still dry and so was our bivy gear. The feeling was, "Thank God! I want to crawl into my bivy and never come out." In the morning it was still slightly drizzling and we didn't want to go down the slabs, so we went back up to the shoulder and followed the hikers' trail to the Valley. We were pretty embarrassed for the first month or two.

## Analysis

Chris's comment, "It's just a hikers' trail…" hit the bull's-eye. Even the climbing guidebooks devote no more than a brief phrase to this descent, but everything changes in the dark and the fog. Information is readily available: The standard 1:24000 USGS maps, Google Maps, SuperTopo, and lots of trip reports on the web show the trail to the summit in enough detail to get you headed in the general direction when you top out. Chris is right again stating that a compass is valuable, but it needs to be paired with a map, whether on paper or accurately stored in your brain.

Never trust what appear to be cairns in Yosemite or other national parks. *(Editor's Note: They are invaluable in some locations, such as the White Mountains in NH.)* The NPS does not construct them, and they often lead nowhere. When it gets down to searching by Braille in the fog without falling off the end of the earth, then it's time to rope up. This is not just for safety, but also for navigation. Leave the belayer in one spot as your reference point and explore in an arc. Even when not roped up, it helps to explore from a point you can always go back to; this is standard advice for hikers anywhere.

Chris confessed, in hindsight, "Looking back, it was a foolish decision to try the climb under the circumstances, but at the time our trip was coming to an end, and we didn't want to leave the Valley without achieving one of our objectives." The decision to climb in view of the forecast wasn't necessarily foolish, but going with marginal ability to escape or to survive an injury stranded on the wall in the predicted conditions was cutting it close. They were pretty well prepared for the dark and the weather they actually encountered, but they would have been better off with a few more items, such as warm/waterproof gloves, one more warm body-layer, and a second, light-weight rope for full pitch rappels.

Everyone goes light these days, but October is storm season, and the summit of Half Dome, at 9000 feet, is not the Valley floor. If this storm had hit them a couple of hours earlier on the wall and/or if it had been just a bit colder, they would have been in a far worse predicament. That's a lot of "ifs", but consider this: On October 3, 1994, at 2200, it began to rain in the Valley. By the time the storm cleared, we had rescued 13 climbers from El Cap, and Half Dome looked like Greenland. It all started on the same day of the year and one hour after Chris and Apple reached the top. (You'll find that case in ANAM 1995.)

This isn't the first time climbers have called for directions from the Half Dome summit and not the only place descent confusion occurs. See, for example, Royal Arches, April 10, 2007, in ANAM 2008. (Source: Chris Tomasetti and John Dill, NPS Ranger, Yosemite National Park)

*(Editor's Note: This is what we call a "near miss." If the climbers had become stranded or had needed to be rescued, we would have included the data in the Tables.)*

## FALL ON ROCK, PROTECTION PULLED OUT and INADEQUATE PROTECTION, EXCEEDING ABILITIES
### California, Tahquitz Rock

On October 19, Sean was leading the first pitch of "The Blank" route on Tahquitz when he fell. The route began at a large ledge and access to the ledge was via easy 3rd-class on the right side of the ledge. The back of the ledge dropped off 20 feet or more to a relatively flat area on the talus field below the rock. The ledge was large enough that the climbers felt comfortable relaxing, walking around and having a snack while waiting for the party ahead of them on the route to get underway on the second pitch before starting to climb.

The climbers did not anchor before Sean began to lead. Sean started up the pitch a couple of feet and placed a nut in the crack (finger sized and thin) and clipped to it using a quick draw. The nut was well slotted in the crack. Sean was having difficulty with the pitch and fell twice with no failure of the nut. Then Sean managed to get high enough that his waist was approximately level with the nut. He had his right foot smeared to the right and his left foot suddenly lost friction. He noticed the nut come out of the crack as he fell toward his left. Sean hit the ledge and either bounced or rolled off of the back side, falling to the flat area about 20 feet below. Rick, the belayer, reported that Sean seemed to have been "catapulted" off of the rock rather than falling more or less straight down, as he would have expected. Rick was pulled off of the ledge and landed about five feet from Sean.

Sean had severe pain in his right ribcage and difficulty breathing. Rick had a large laceration above his right eye. Both climbers had multiple cuts and scrapes.

The climbers above heard the commotion and rappelled down to help. One of those climbers, Evan, stated that he was an emergency medical technician and began to help. Soon other climbers were on the scene and plans were being made to get Sean and Rick off of the mountain. Sean was able to walk around, with much pain, and the plan was to secure Rick to one of the Stokes litters that had fortunately been stashed in the area and carry him down. Someone made a 911 call on his or her cell phone. Idyllwild Fire Dept arrived on the scene some time later and examined both injured climbers. Their team recommended both climbers be extracted by helicopter due to the unknown extent of Rick's injuries and because Sean was showing symptoms of a collapsed lung.

Both climbers were evacuated to the hospital. Rick was released that night, and Sean was released two days later. Fortunately, Rick had not suffered a concussion but did have two apparently non-serious fractures in his skull and a possible sprained wrist as well as a deep cut at one knee. Sean had four fractured ribs and a collapsed lung. As of four weeks since the incident both climbers are recovering well and will probably not have any serious long-term consequences from their injuries.

## Analysis

Sean is an experienced climber with over 22 years of traditional rock climbing experience. Rick had been climbing for seven months. Both climbers were wearing helmets.

The climbers should have anchored the belayer. Sean believed that as long as a good piece of protection could be placed before proceeding too far, an anchor would not be necessary; in fact he never gave much if any thought to anchoring due to the seemingly large area of the ledge. Even if there had been no effective way to anchor, the protection placed should have been as bombproof as possible. One way to do this would have been to back up the first piece and to use a camming device instead of a nut.

It is possible that the nut would not have popped out if a runner had been used to extend it out instead of a standard quickdraw. Quickdraws are remarkably easy to lift with very little side movement of the rope.

Sean should also have checked the security of the nut after having fallen on it twice. It is possible that the nut became partially dislodged while holding the previous two falls.

And finally, a climber having enough difficulty so that he or she falls twice, and is still very close to the base of the route, should seriously consider backing off and climbing something else.

Experienced climbers sometimes become complacent about some of the basic safety procedures used in climbing, such as anchoring the belayer at the base of the route. It is actually not very often that the actual technical climbing starts on absolutely level ground, and it is not unheard of for belayers to be lifted off their feet while arresting a leader fall.

In this case both climbers were fortunate. If the area below the ledge had been covered with sharp rocks instead of being relatively flat, unlike most of the surrounding terrain, which is very rough, it is likely that their injuries would have been much more serious if not fatal. (Source: Shawn Lonergan)

*(Editor's Note: We received two reports from Mount Shasta, one of which was a fatality that occurred when a woman (35) was unable to self-arrest. She and her two climbing companions were not wearing helmets. A brief report found on mountainproject.com stated that two teenagers were climbing at Foothill Crag—*

*near Ojai—when one of them fell 45 feet to the ground because the climbing rope burned through a webbing anchor as he was being lowered. He had not threaded the rope through carabiners, apparently. While his injuries were serious,—including fractured pelvis and ribs and a punctured lung.)*

## AVALANCHE
### Colorado, Little Bear Peak, Standard Hourglass Route

On January 10 around 1100, a male (22) and his sister (20) were climbing Little Bear Peak via the Standard West Ridge Hourglass Route. Weather conditions for several days had been mostly cloudy to partly cloudy, snowing (19-36 inches), and windy (out of the west and southwest, 8-41 mph). As the two climbers were traversing the south side of the West Ridge, just west of the base of the Hourglass Couloir, they triggered a large slab avalanche. The crown was approximately 500 feet across, a foot or more deep and the slide descended approximately 1000 vertical feet, including a drop over a 100-foot cliff. The male reported that his sister was eight feet behind him when he found himself "rag dolling" down the south-facing slope of the West Ridge. Before losing consciousness, he recalled going over the cliff.

The male awoke buried to his waist with a laceration to his forehead, three broken ribs, and a punctured lung. He was on the edge of a debris field in the cirque above Little Bear Lake approximately 1000 feet below where the avalanche began. His titanium ice ax's adze had been snapped off and the pick had been bent 30 degrees from its original position. He called out for his sister, but there was no response. He dug himself out, and began searching for his sister. He probed the debris field with his ice axe for over an hour. With no sign of his sister, he decided to go for help.

He ascended the West Ridge and descended to their last camp at Lake Como. He reached the camp around sunset. On January 11, after regaining strength and sleeping for a short period, he descended the Lake Como trail on skis to the point where he acquired cell phone contact and called 911. At 0830, Alamosa County Sheriff's Office dispatched the Alamosa Volunteer Search and Rescue team to search for a lost hiker. A command post was set-up at the Lake Como access trailhead. Because of deep snow, cold temperatures, and the potential for a short window of response time to the patient, SAR personnel requested Flight For Life helicopter support. Lifeguard Four was dispatched from Pueblo, Colorado.

At 1100, a two-man hasty team was flown to Lake Como from the Lake Como trailhead, and a three man hasty team was dispatched from the command post to ascend the access road on ATV's until the snow depth stopped their progress. At Lake Como, the helicopter delivered hasty team observed a single set of tracks leading down the couloir used to access the West Ridge on Little Bear Peak. About the same time as the helicopter insertion, the ATV team made contact with the injured climber. He was evacuated via ATV to the command post where he was airlifted via Flight For Life to the San Luis Valley Medical Center in Alamosa.

Conditions over the next several days prevented search and recovery of the woman. Her remains were ultimately recovered on June 24, by a team of four Alamosa Volunteer Search and Rescue technicians and a dog handler and recovery dog provided by SARDOC (Search and Rescue Dogs of Colorado).

**Analysis**

Both subjects had technical alpine experience in Colorado, Alaska and South America. Just the previous spring, they had completed a successful summit of Denali together; however, this experience did not make them immune to the dangers that exist any time people enter potential avalanche terrain. At the hospital, the young man stated to a SAR interviewer that after the avalanche, the snow was "whumpfing" in the access couloir during his descent to Lake Como. Earlier in the morning before the slide, the snowpack was more stable as they ascended, but as they crossed over the ridge into the slabs that were affected by solar radiation and wind effects, they were unaware of the changes in the snow-pack's stability or the potential danger of descending the access couloir later in the day. Neither subject had an avalanche beacon, probe or shovel with them; however, because of the massive scale of the slide and the depth of the deceased subject, none of these items would have changed the outcome. Avalanche terrain avoidance would have been the only method of mitigating this accident. (Source: Edited from a report submitted by Kevin Wright, President, Alamosa Volunteer Search and Rescue)

## FALL OR SLIP ON ICE, INADEQUATE PROTECTION
### Colorado, Rocky Mountain National Park, The Squid

On Sunday March 2, a female climber (32) and her partners were climbing the Squid (WI5) located above Emerald Lake and considered by many to be the most spectacular single ice pitch in Colorado. While "running it out" to the top of the route she fell, her ice screw arresting her fall (approximately 35 feet), but not before hitting a ledge and landing on a rock shelf, suffering serious injuries to her pelvis and lower leg. Her partners were able to lower her to the ground and contacted park dispatch by cell phone.

Park personnel responded, provided medical care, and lowered her approximately 120 meters down a steep snow slope using a belay. They then skied out approximately two miles to a waiting ambulance at the Bear Lake trailhead. She was taken to Estes Park Medical Center, and then transported by ambulance to Boulder Community Hospital. (Source: The National Park Service Morning Report, March 12)

## STRANDED, DARKNESS, INADEQUATE EQUIPMENT – NO HEADLAMP, INADEQUATE CLOTHING, EXCEEDING ABILITIES
### Colorado, Eldorado Canyon State Park, Yellow Spur

Around 2:00 p.m. on the afternoon of March 9, I (Nandu Thibeault, 23) and my partner (19) started on Yellow Spur, a seven-pitch, 5.9-rock climb on Redgarden Wall. This was the second multi-pitch traditional climb I've done, so my rope management and racking skills were inefficient. My partner has only been climbing outdoors a few times, so I was leading every pitch. It wasn't until the third pitch that I realized I had forgotten my headlamp.

As I set up the belay on the summit I watched the sun go down, then watched as night slowly crept in as I literally pulled my partner up the crux pitch. I would have set up the belay before the 5.6 arête, but we had only one cordalette so I had to sling my rope around the peak. When my partner finally arrived, I coiled the rope and I had him read the descent information from the Mountain Project printout we had brought with us. We only had about 15 more minutes before it was too dark to read, and I did my best to memorize all of the descent information.

We began to rap in the dark and I had no clue where to go. There were trees and fins of rock, notches, and gullies everywhere; I couldn't remember what the printout said. I checked all the trees for slings or rope burn. I scrambled and checked all the rocks for anchors.

We down-climbed a gulley for about 150 yards only to meet a vertical drop. After this recon, I realized that we would be spending the night in our T-shirts. We climbed back up the gulley and made a bed out of pine branches on a small low angle pad of rock. The wind forced us to relocate throughout the night, and we tried a number of techniques to stay warm. It was a pretty miserable experience, but as soon as we found the anchors the next morning I was thankful for the lessons learned and ready to attack another multi-itch climb!

### Analysis

Nadu admitted that Yellow Spur was his second traditional climb and that his partner had limited multi-pitch experience. Given these admissions, it may have been more prudent to choose a less demanding and committing rock climb, especially given the time of day. A small fanny or daypack with headlamp, extra layers, hat, energy bars, and water may have prevented a night out or made the night out more comfortable. (Source: Edited from an email by Nadu Thibeault)

## FALL OR SLIP ON ROCK, MISCOMMUNICATION
### Colorado, Eldorado Canyon State Park, Wind Tower

On May 4, Lon Abbott (45) and Avery McGill (25) were climbing Recon (5.6) on the Wind Tower. Both men were experienced climbers and wearing helmets. They had been leading, then rappelling all day. During the afternoon Abbott fell from the anchors on top of the first pitch, stopping about 20-30 feet below the belay ledge. Reports suggest that Abbott was tied into the rope while it was under tension from the anchor at the top of the first pitch as it passed through the chains (or the injured climber's gear), down and through a few more pieces, then down to the base of the climb. Abbott had called, "Off belay!" and was not on belay when he fell.

At the on-set of the fall, McGill thought there was rockfall and took shelter underneath an outcrop. When he realized Abbott was falling, he tried to grab the rope but couldn't hold on to it. He suffered a hand injury, suggesting that Abbott fell onto his hand.

Luckily for Abbott, the rope got caught or twisted in the first piece of protection on the pitch, which appeared to "arrest" the fall keeping him from tumbling further down the 4th class slope.

Quick action from climbers in the area saved Abbott's life. He was air lifted to Denver Health Medical Center where his injuries were assessed and included two broken vertebrae, broken ankles, five broken ribs, a broken shoulder blade and a concussion. He is expected to recover.

### Analysis

Experienced climbers will often keep the leader on belay when he reaches the top of a pitch, even if he says, "Off belay." This is followed by giving a few feet of slack and then tying a knot in the rope on the brake side of the belay device until it becomes evident that the leader is tied off to the anchor.

Since Abbott and McGill had been leading and rappelling all day, they may not have talked about changing what they had been doing. Instead, McGill may have assumed that they would continue, which leads to the speculation that after leading the pitch Abbott, decided to lower instead of rappelling, but forgot to communicate this with McGill.

There is also some speculation that the "off belay" command did not come from Abbott, but from another party in the immediate area. Whatever happened, it's a good time to remind us all that we should always communicate with our partners. (Source: Edited from entries on mountainproject.com and a rockymountainnews.com websites)

## FALL OR SLIP ON ROCK, PULLED LOOSE ROCK OFF — FALLING ROCK HIT CLIMBING PARTNER
### Colorado, Eldorado Canyon State Park, Doub-Griffith

During the afternoon on May 27, two experienced climbers, Chris Lee

(38) and Chris Klinga (25) were attempting Doub-Griffith, a 5.11c 3-pitch traditional route that starts from a small ledge 150 feet above the base of Redgarden Wall. As Lee was climbing, he inadvertently pulled a large, table-sized flake free from the wall. The rock hit Lee in the abdomen, causing both Lee and the flake to fall. Using a Cinch auto-locking belay device, Klinga stopped Lee's fall after which Klinga was struck with the rock that had broken loose, injuring both his legs. Lee was able to get to the ground and walk out on his own.

Rocky Mountain Fire and Rocky Mountain Rescue climbed to Klinga's location and set up an evacuation system. The team evacuated Klinga off of the rock ledge and down to the road. The evacuation included a 150-foot vertical and a 300-foot scree lowers. Klinga was transported to St. Anthony's Central by a medical helicopter.

### Analysis

Loose rock is relatively common objective hazard. Climbers should be wary of loose rock by testing handholds, avoiding sections of loose rock, and not being in a direct line of potential rockfall from above. Climbers should also ask themselves, "What if?" In this case, what sorts of precautions can be taken by the belayer to protect the leader if the belayer is incapacitated during a leader fall? (Source: From rockymountainnews and bouldercounty. org websites and Aram Attarian)

### FALL ON ROCK, PROTECTION PULLED OUT
**Colorado, Eldorado Canyon State Park, Bastille, Werk Supp**

On July 14, Preston Brennan (47), an experienced climber, and his partner were climbing Werk Supp, a 5.9 route located on the Bastille. Witnesses noted that while on the first part of the climb, Preston had placed two nuts and was working on the third for quite some time. He placed another about ten or so feet above the third. While placing the fifth piece, he lost his grip and fell, hitting the left side of his forehead on rock and losing consciousness for the rest of the fall, since he made no sound and came down "like a rag doll". Two of the nuts pulled. He fell at least 50 feet suffering serious brain injuries, which eventually led to his death a week later. (Source: H. Urie, *The Daily Camera*, July 19, and a series of postings on mountainproject.com)

### FALL OR SLIP ON ROCK, CLIMBING ALONE
**Colorado, Eldorado Canyon State Park, Bastille, Werk Supp**

Michael Hankins (47), an experienced and highly regarded climber from Oklahoma set out to solo Werk Supp (5.9) on July 22. He fell when he was 50 feet into the climb. Hankins was airlifted to St. Anthony Central Hospital in Denver. He suffered compound fractures to both his legs and left arm, a broken pelvis and brain injury. He later died from his injuries.

## Analysis

Dave Secunda, who is a member of the Colorado Mountain Rescue Group, said Hankins was climbing using one of the most technically challenging methods—solo climbing—without the aid of ropes or harnesses. "Soloing is not the way that most people climb," he said. "It is an elite, high-end part of the sport. He was at the absolute extreme of the spectrum of risk that climbers take. There is no backup system. Climbing [has some inherent risks], and I think we all, as climbers, embrace those potential risks when we go out there. I think the right response is to pause and extend our thoughts and prayers to the people involved. (Source: H. Urie, *The Daily Camera*—July 23, mountainproject.com, and Dave Secunda, Rocky Mountain Rescue Group)

## FALL ON ROCK, POOR PRACTICE – HOOKED FINGERS THROUGH BOLT RING
### Colorado, Red Rock Canyon Open Space, Rethinking the Ethics

Rethinking the Ethics (5.10a) is a 45-foot, four-bolt sport climb located on the Ripple Wall. The climb culminates at a two-bolt anchor beneath the top of an arch. In late September, a male climber was leading this route and upon reaching the two-bolt anchor, hooked his fingers into the ring to pull up rope. In his attempt to pull up the rope, he lost his hold and fell with the rope behind his leg. This action caused him to flip upside down and strike the back of his head on the rock, causing a concussion requiring an evacuation.

### Analysis

Upon reaching the top of the route, climbers clip the rope into both of the top anchors then girth hitch two slings to the harness through the belay/rappel loop and attach a locking carabiner to the end of each sling. Each sling is then clipped to each bolt on the anchor, no longer relying on the belayer or the climbing rope. At this point a figure-8-on-a bight is tied and clipped into either a carabiner on the harness or into the anchor, which prevents losing the end of the rope when it's untied in the next step. Next, the original tie-in knot is untied from the harness and passed through the rap rings on the anchor. More rope is pulled up from the belayer in order to rappel using both sides of the rope making sure both ends of the rope reach the ground. This technique eliminates unnecessary wear on the fixed gear, which has been an acknowledged problem at Red Rock Canyon. (Source: from a posting on mountainproject.com)

## FALL ON ROCK, PLACED NO PROTECTION, EXCEEDING ABILITIES
### Colorado, Eldorado Canyon State Park, Grandmother's Challenge

On October 8, Kevin (51), an experienced climber, and his wife started the first pitch of Grandmother's Challenge (5.10c), a two-pitch climb on

Redgarden Wall. The first pitch is rated 5.8. Kevin was approximately 30 feet above the ground with no protection in place and slipped, landing feet first on a large ledge then losing balance and falling feet first again onto the ground. At least one ankle was fractured and the other severely sprained if not also fractured. Kevin also complained of lower back pain when rescue arrived. (Source: From an accident report completed by Chris Darr.)
*(Editor's Note: According to statistics kept by the Rocky Mountain Rescue Group, there were 20 reports of injured rock climbers within the group's response area last year. From 2002 to 2006, the group averaged 27 calls a year for injured climbers, with an average of nine responses a year in Eldorado Canyon State Park.)*

## FALL ON ROCK
### Colorado, Black Canyon of the Gunnison National Park, Stoned Oven
On Monday, October 20, Irishman Michael Walsh (30) and his two partners were attempting the Stoned Oven Route (5.11d), a 13 pitch, Grade V rock climb located on the North Chasm View Wall. Around 11:00 a.m., Walsh was approximately 600 feet above the ground when he fell 30 to 40 feet while leading the fourth pitch of the route. He fell hard enough to shatter his helmet. He was disoriented and appeared to be suffering from a life-threatening head injury.

Walsh's partners lowered him to the floor of the canyon, and one of them ascended the 1,700-foot Cruise Gully route by scrambling and using an ascender on fixed ropes. After seeking help from the others, he gathered equipment, including sleeping bags, warm clothing and head lamps, and returned down the Cruise Gully to assist Walsh and the other partner.

At 1:30 PM a park visitor came to the North Rim Ranger Station to report the accident. The individual reporting the accident was not a member of Walsh's party, but she had been at the North Rim Campground when a member from Walsh's party appeared seeking assistance.

A hasty team responded immediately, descending the technically demanding Cruise Gully. Although their response time was slowed slightly by rain, the team reached Walsh just after 5:00 p.m. Due to the nature of Walsh's injuries, the park SAR team, assisted by members of Western State SAR, began a rescue operation despite the approaching darkness. A park SAR team member was lowered from the rim to the canyon floor in the area of the Hallucinogen Wall route (5.10, A3+). A litter carry was made from the base of the Stoned Oven route to the haul lines, and Walsh and a rescuer were then hauled 1,500 vertical feet to the canyon rim, arriving there around 11:00 p.m. Walsh was then flown to a hospital via air ambulance. The entire rescue operation took less than nine hours from the time of first notification to its conclusion.

## Analysis

A good example of the ability of a climbing party to initiate a self-rescue and the effectiveness of a well-trained SAR team. (Source: Steve Winslow, District Ranger in the NPS Morning Report for October 28, and www.firerescuemagazine.com)

## FALL ON ROCK – RAPPEL ERROR, INADEQUATE PROTECTION– OLD ANCHOR WEBBING PARTED, INADEQUATE EQUIPMENT – NO HEADLAMPS
### Kentucky, Red River Gorge, Emerald City

On November 4, the bodies of Benjamin Strohmeier (18) and Laura Fletcher (18) were found near the base of a climbing route in an area of USDA Forest Service land, known in the climbing community as "Emerald City". They were found fifty feet below a belay station used to set up a second pitch rappel from a top anchor. They had apparently fallen from a small ledge at this belay station. The fall was essentially vertical. There were no witnesses to this incident.

After the coroner took photos, the victims were freed from the rope and climbing gear and removed from the scene. The climbing gear and the victims' possessions were taken into evidence by the Forest Service and upon examination of all the evidence, the cause and sequencing of the incident was unanimously agreed upon, the details of which follow.

About 4:00 p.m. on November 3, Strohmeier was observed leading a trad line directly above the incident scene. The eyewitness, who was standing about 300 yards away at the road, did not see Strohmeier's belayer, as trees obscured his view. It is assumed that Fletcher was his belayer. This may have been the last time anyone else saw either of the victims alive.

The climbing pair rappelled down to a lower belay station on a small ledge 50 feet above the base of the climb. The base consists of rock-strewn earth directly below this lower belay station. The belay station ledge is small but was of sufficient size for the pair to stand together, hands free.

At the belay station, the pair found an anchor system consisting of a 36-inch length of 1-inch tubular nylon webbing threaded through an aluminum rappel ring and two hanger brackets. The webbing ends were joined using a water knot. Although the hangers and bolts were heavily rusted, subsequent inspection showed that they would probably have supported the load of a rappelling climber. However, the webbing was so badly weathered and deteriorated that it could not and, in fact, did not support that load.

The sequence of events was thus: Strohmeier clipped a quickdraw onto the belay loop of his harness, clipped another quickdraw onto the end of the first one, and then clipped the distal carabiner of the two chained quickdraws onto the webbing. He did not clip into the rappel ring. This action essentially tethered him into the anchor system, which would have kept him safe from falling off the ledge if the anchor system had been in good condition and the webbing had not failed.

Fletcher at or near the same time started to rig for a rappel to the ground from the belay station. She fed a 60-meter dynamic, bi-pattern climbing rope through the rappel ring on the webbing and pulled it through until the middle of the rope was near the rappel ring and the two ends of the rope were hanging down the cliff. Fletcher threaded both sides of the rope exiting the rappel ring into a Petzl Reverso belay/rappel device. She then captured the two bights of rope in the Reverso and the Reverso's larger loop with a locking carabiner and clipped this assemblage to her belay loop. She had now set herself up to rappel from the belay station, although she did not use any type of backup.

It is important to note here that at some point prior to Fletcher starting her rappel, Strohmeier took the fatal step of clipping his distal carabiner on his chained quickdraws not only onto the webbing, but also onto the rope between the top of Fletcher's Reverso and the point where it threaded through the rappel ring. It is possible that he did this intentionally for some unknown reason, or it could have been done unintentionally, due to diminished light. He was now clipped both to the webbing and this bight of rope.

Fletcher stepped off the ledge to rappel and weighted the rope and anchor system. At or shortly after this point in time, the webbing experienced a catastrophic tensile failure. The rappel ring was freed from the webbing causing Fletcher to fall. And, because Strohmeier was clipped into the bight of rope coming out of Fletcher's Reverso, he was yanked off the ledge by her weight. Both of them experienced a free-fall of about 50 feet to the ground.

The victims were found with about six feet of doubled rope joining the two climbers together between her Reverso and his distal carabiner. Unfortunately, when the rope was cut to remove the victims, the rappel ring fell out of the system. Without knowing exactly where this ring was located in the system, the exact cause of the incident might not have been conclusive. However, close examination of the Coroner's photos taken before the rope was cut and gear was removed clearly shows the rappel ring in the position it had to be in relative to the other gear for this incident to occur as described above.

## Analysis

At 3:53 p.m. on November 3, the Jackson Airport Weather Station (approximately 20 miles from the incident scene) reported a temperature of 71.1 degrees F, wind NW at 4.6 mph, and skies clear. Sunset at location was at 5:53 p.m. The rock wall at the scene is southwest facing. Cliffs across the road to the west tower over 300 feet above the road and could render the incident scene in significantly diminished light even before sunset.

The human factor cause of the incident was an error in judgment. Rather than leave gear behind at the anchor station—gear such as a runner and/or carabiners, both of which the two climbers had with them—they elected to trust their lives to an ancient, weathered piece of webbing.

Another possible contributing factor is that because only the leader, Strohmeier, was seen topping out and Fletcher had not started climbing this route by 4:00 p.m., it may be that the climbing pair did not start the rappel until it was relatively dark. No headlamp or flashlight was found on or near the victims. Without means to light their way or illuminate the gear present on the wall, this could account for the pair's decision to trust webbing, which may have seemed to be in better condition than it actually was. (Source: Richard Weber, Team Leader—Red River Gorge Mountain Rescue Team For USDA Forest Service Law Enforcement)

## AVALANCHE, CLIMBING ALONE, POOR POSITION
### New Hampshire, Mount Washington, Huntington Ravine, Odell Gully

At 9:20 p.m. on January 18 the USFS Snow Rangers were informed that a solo climber (39-male) from Lewiston, ME, was overdue from his climb in Huntington Ravine. He had signed into the winter climbers' register at Pinkham Notch with a plan of climbing Central Gully. According to his friends who reported him overdue, he had experience in many gullies in Huntington Ravine and had talked about Odell Gully as another option for his day.

A team searched the access routes into Huntington Ravine between 10:00 p.m. and midnight on the 18th. Due to snow stability concerns, search teams didn't enter avalanche terrain until first light the next day to begin searching Huntington Ravine. Shortly after sunrise, the missing climber's body was found in avalanche debris below Odell Gully. The climber was on top of the debris and died as a result of being avalanched out of Odell Gully. He was put in a technical litter, lowered 500 feet to the floor of the Ravine, and transported to Pinkham Notch by the USFS snowcat.

### Analysis

The avalanche danger rating for January 18 was posted High for all forecast areas in Huntington Ravine. The definition of this rating states natural and human triggered avalanches are likely, unstable slabs are likely on a variety of aspects and slope angles, and travel in avalanche terrain is not recommended. This rating was based on active wind-loading of new snow that had been accumulating since snowfall began around 4:00 a.m. that morning. Winds associated with the storm began out of the south before shifting to the west around 12:00 p.m. and increasing to the 60-70 mph range with a peak gust on the summit out of the west of 86 mph at 5:42 p.m. Recorded snow totals from this storm were 3.9 inches at Hermit Lake and 3.1 inches on the summit of Mount Washington with locally higher amounts. The density of the snow was lighter at the beginning and became heavier through the day, with an average density at Hermit Lake of 12.8 percent

Odell is a popular climbing route with sections of snow and grade 2 and 3 ice. It faces E and ENE and has multiple avalanche start zones. The winds associated with this storm were ideal for loading Odell by starting out of the south and wrapping around to the west. It is believed that the climber triggered the avalanche, though this is not conclusive. The size of the avalanche was classified as D2R3. D2 refers to the destructive force of an avalanche and means that it could bury, injure or kill a person. R3 means that the avalanche was medium sized relative to its normal path. Evidence of natural avalanche activity from this storm was observed on similar aspects.

It is easy to look at incidents such as this one and make simple judgments on the victim's actions. Undoubtedly, most people would change their plans when a current avalanche forecast projects avalanches as being likely on their intended route. Nonetheless, the majority of our avalanche fatalities and serious accidents have occurred in areas that were posted with High Avalanche Danger. This contrasts with the general trend around the world where the majority of accidents happen under a Considerable rating. Though this accident did happen in an area that was rated as High, it could have occurred under a rating of Low, Moderate or Considerable.

Solo climbers are often exposed to a greater degree of risk than roped teams. In this incident, the size of the avalanche probably had little to do with the outcome. Had the victim triggered an isolated pocket of unstable snow, as is feasible under a rating of Low, the end result would likely have been similar. Although climbing roped with a partner cannot save you from all mountain dangers, it does substantially increase the size of the safety net if used properly. When approaching a suspect area, the best use of a rope incorporates solid protection that is located to the side of the pocket or snowfield in question. This is by no means a failsafe tactic, but it does provide some extra security should one be knocked off one's feet by snow, falling ice, etc.

Secondly, it is worth noting that the US 5-Scale Danger Rating System is a continuum and not a series of five distinct categories without overlap. Within any particular rating there is also a range and we frequently try to discuss this in the daily avalanche advisory. When the victim passed the Harvard Cabin, the avalanche advisory stated the following: "N-facing aspects will be the first to move up into the High rating with E and S-facing aspects to follow as the winds shift." Armed with this data, it would be prudent to consider the other options if one was determined to climb a gully in the ravine that day. By the time the victim was approaching the start of the climb, the winds had begun their forecasted shift and Odell Gully was in the direct lee of wind loading. Farther to the right, gullies such as North and Damnation likely had less loading occurring and would have had smaller sections of suspect snow to navigate.

Mountain skills are complex and require a high degree of technical training in a variety of disciplines. This climber had a lot of experience climbing in Huntington including numerous solo ascents of gullies. He was well prepared to deal with the weather and steep mountain terrain found in Huntington Ravine. As is often the case in avalanche accidents, it appears that technical climbing experience surpassed knowledge of mountain snowpack. In addition, the victim was not carrying any avalanche safety equipment. Though it did not make a difference in this scenario, carrying this equipment provides an additional tool should the unthinkable occur. Even if climbing alone, this gear can help out when things go bad. Other climbers in the area could locate a person if he were buried while wearing a beacon. With this said, self-sufficiency is paramount in avalanche rescue, so having a party of two or more is needed.

### FALL ON SNOW – UNABLE TO SELF-ARREST
### New Hampshire, Mount Washington, Huntington Ravine

On January 25, a party of four was ascending the Fan in Huntington Ravine when one of them (38) fell and slid into two other people in his party, causing them to fall as well. One of three involved in the fall was unable to self-arrest on the icy surface and tumbled about 50 feet before hitting a rock. He sustained a soft tissue injury to his left thigh. The patient's party was able to assist him down to the Harvard Cabin and notified the caretaker of the incident and requested assistance. A Snow Ranger assessed his injuries and transported the patient to Pinkham Notch via snowmobile.

### FALL ON SNOW, UNABLE TO SELF-ARREST, INADEQUATE EQUIPMENT – NO HEADLAMPS
### New Hampshire, Mount Washington, Huntington Ravine

On January 26, a novice climber (44) and his partner started up Odell Gully around 3:00 p.m. on Saturday afternoon. After completing the main ice climbing section, they traversed to the east to begin their descent. Neither had headlamps with them and darkness complicated their descent. According to the party, they were in the lower section of the Escape Hatch when one of them lost his footing and began a sliding fall. Unable to self-arrest, he slid approximately 150 feet before slamming into a tree and stopping. The fall resulted in injuries to his back and legs. The two were able to get to the Harvard Cabin under their own power where local guides and the caretaker provided assistance to the climber and notified the USFS Snow Rangers who arrived at the Harvard Cabin around 9:30 p.m. The patient was reassessed, immobilized on a backboard and transported via snowcat to Pinkham Notch where he was transferred to an ambulance and brought to the hospital. We later learned that he had fractured two vertebrae in his lower back and had numerous sprains and contusions

**Analysis**

This was the third sliding fall injury in three days. All of them would likely have been prevented with a quick self-arrest. The surface that all of these occurred on was a very hard, icy snowpack from the January thaw, which is difficult to stop on, so if a fall isn't arrested immediately, one will get out of control fast.

In each of these incidents, the parties involved did a good job getting to the Harvard Cabin under their own power.

## FALL ON SNOW – LOSS OF CONTROL ON VOLUNTARY GLISSADE
### New Hampshire, Mount Washington, Lion's Head Winter route

On March 3, a group of mountaineers (ages unknown) were glissading Lion's Head Winter Route when one of them lost control and fell down approximately 75-100 feet through the trees to the bottom of the steep section of trail. Along the way, he hit some trees and came to a stop against a large stump.

USFS Snow Rangers were notified of the incident by a hiker who had been sent to Hermit Lake to get help. Although below the steepest section of trail, the patient was found in terrain sufficiently steep to warrant belaying the litter downhill until the flat section of trail. From here he was sledded to the junction of the Winter Route and the Huntington Ravine Winter Access Trail, then transported via snowmobile and haul sled to Pinkham Notch Visitor Center.

**Analysis**

The Winter Route on Lion's Head is a steep mountaineering route that requires the ability to self-arrest in the event of a fall. Glissading was a reasonable descent option given the soft snow conditions on this day.

## AVALANCHE, POOR POSITION
### New Hampshire, Mount Washington, Huntington Ravine

During the afternoon of March 30, two climbers (ages unknown) emerged from North Gully onto the more open slopes above the gully. After simul-climbing the gully's midsection, they unroped and began to climb the snow up toward Ball Crag. They identified an area of potentially unstable snow and decided to move off to the side of the slope and travel one at a time. One of the climbers triggered an avalanche, but neither were caught or carried in the slide. Unsure of the outcome below, they quickly worked their way around the ravine and descended the Escape Hatch to see if anyone needed help.

A second party of two experienced ice climbers (ages 32 and 26) believed the first party had already finished the climb so they began the first ice pitch. The leader arrived at a fixed belay above the first pitch of ice and clipped his rope to the anchor with a carabiner. He was in the process of backing up the anchor when the avalanche came from above. At this point, the anchor was serving as a piece of protection and he was essentially still on lead.

The avalanche carried the leader down over the top of the first pitch of ice. The belayer was unanchored at the bottom and was lifted upslope and into the ice. He was able to maintain control of the belay and the fixed anchor held, resulting in approximately a 50-foot fall for the leader. Both climbers were shaken up, sore, and had damaged their helmets in the fall. Examinations by Snow Rangers at the scene found no serious injuries. The climbers stayed overnight at the Harvard Cabin, where the following morning they reported general soreness but no other injuries.

## Analysis

The weather leading up this incident is an example of a classic setup for an avalanche cycle. On March 28, Mount Washington received 6.4 inches of 7.8-percent density snow. Hermit Lake recorded almost eight inches from the same weather system. Friday night and Saturday the winds wrapped from the W to the NNW and increased in velocity before falling again on Sunday. Evidence of natural avalanche activity was visible Sunday morning in several locations, including Hillman's Highway, South Gully, Raymond's Cataract, the Lion Head Summer Trail, the East Snowfields of the summit cone, and in small snowfields that descend from Lion Head toward the Tuckerman Ravine Trail. Avalanche danger for North Gully on Sunday was rated Moderate.

Fortunately this incident turned out well for all parties involved. It very easily could have been worse. Several lessons can be gleaned from this incident:

- *Choice of route.* Five of eight gullies in Huntington had Low avalanche danger while three (North, Damnation, and Central) had Moderate. In regards to snow stability, choosing anther gully would have been a safer option.
- *Climbing below another party.* Ice climbing below others always carries additional risk, whether it's from falling ice and rocks or avalanches. The party that was hit by the avalanche understood that climbing under another party was a bad choice. They thought that the gully was clear and that it was safe to start up. It is difficult to see the entire gully from the base of the ice, but a short walk to a better vantage point is all that is required for a view of the entire gully.
- *Ongoing stability assessments.* The top party did a good job of recognizing the unstable snow at the top of the climb. Traveling one at a time off to

the side of the area in question helped prevent them from being caught in the avalanche. Had they wanted to protect themselves further, they could have roped up again and climbed to the top using belays and protection. *(Editor's Note: During the spring skiing season in Tuckerman, there were several falls that required Snow Rangers, members of the Mount Washington Volunteer Ski Patrol, and AMC caretakers to assist with lowers and medical conditions. Sometimes skiers put themselves in poor positions that can and often do result in being struck by falling ice or falling into moats.*

*The source for all the incidents on Mount Washington is the Tuckerman Ravine website and conversations with Justin Preisendorfer, Snow Ranger/Backcountry & Wilderness Supervisor)*

## FALL ON ROCK
### New Hampshire, Cathedral Ledge

In August, Christopher Townsend (27), an experienced climber from Cambridge, MA, took a twenty-foot fall that left him hanging unconscious on his rope for about two minutes. He walked out of the hospital later in the day "courtesy of his helmet."

*(Editor's Note: No other rock climbing incidents were reported by the Mountain Rescue Service located in North Conway. Rick Wilcox, the President of MRS, indicated in a phone conversation that there were probably more incidents, but unless rescue is required, climbers tend to leave without telling about their mishaps.)*

## FALLS ON ROCK (16), FALLING ROCK (1), RAPPEL ERROR (1), INADEQUATE PROTECTION (10), PROTECTION PULLED OUT (4), INADEQUATE BELAY (3), NO HARD HAT (1)
### New York, Mohonk Preserve, Shawangunks, Various Routes

Eighteen reports were submitted for 2008, with dates ranging from March through November. Most incidents occur in July and August.

The average length of the falls was sixteen feet, with seven of them ending up on the ground, mostly because of inadequate protection on the first pitch. The average age of the individuals injured was about 46 and the level of difficulty of the routes averaged 5.7. Eleven of the individuals directly involved were experienced climbers. Most injuries were relatively minor, with sprains and strains being the most common (10).

The rappel error incident was the result of a climbing rope mid-point not being correctly marked. The climber (59), who had 36 years of experience, rappelled off one end of the rope—luckily for only ten feet.

There was one fatality. An experienced climber (58) was on a route rated 5.2-5.3. He climbed out of sight beyond his belayer. He fell past the belayer to the ground. There was a cam and sling behind him, indicating that either he was in the process of setting protection or that it had come out.

This was only the eighth climbing-related fatality in the Shawangunks in the last 45 years. With an estimate of 10,000 climbers visiting this area each year for the past two decades and about 50,000 climbs being attempted annually, this means an extremely low fatality rate. (Source: From reports submitted by Mohonk Preserve)

## FALL OR SLIP ON ROCK, FAILURE TO FOLLOW ROUTE, FATIGUE, DARKNESS
### North Carolina, Linville Gorge Wilderness, Shortoff Mountain, Paradise Alley

On January 12, John Matthew (40) and Nathan Z. (30) both moderately experienced climbers, set off to climb Maginot Line (5.7) and Paradise Alley (5.8) on Shortoff Mountain, located at the south end of the Linville Gorge Wilderness Area. The following description of the events leading up to the incident is described by J. Matthews.

Nathan and I are both WFRs and he is an AMGA TRSM. I have taken the AMGA TRSM course, but have not passed the exam. We have both led groups of youth climbing. We both wear helmets. However, neither of us had been out climbing for a couple of months

We climbed Maginot Line easily and took some time at the top to enjoy the warm January day. By the time we reached the base of Paradise Alley, it was near 4:30 p.m., but we both had headlamps warm layers and felt solid so we set off. Nathan led the first pitch with some difficulty, hanging on the rope a couple of times but taking no falls. I seconded with some difficulty, attributed to mostly fatigue. At the top of pitch one, I consulted the guidebook and set off.

We were using the Lambert/Shull Guide, which marks the route as moving straight up from the belay (the Kelley Guide includes more detail and marks a short blocky scramble to the left before moving left). I climbed straight off the belay and pulled a small roof to gain the face. When I reached the face, I realized I was off-route because the rock was covered in lichen and the climbing difficulty seemed well beyond the 5.8 rating. I knew I needed to move left and I saw what appeared to be a good stance up and to the left. I placed a .3 C4 and started to move up and left towards the stance. I had gone approx 20 feet with protection when I came off the rock.

We were climbing with double ropes and as I fell, one of the ropes caught my leg and flipped me upside down. The total distance of the fall was about 40 feet. The C4 held. Nathan caught my fall, but was pulled upwards about eight feet. When the rope caught my weight, I did a pendulum swing into the rock. The impact was focused on my left shoulder.

By now it was dark. After an initial period of assessment (and a good amount of screaming and yelling), Nathan rigged the ropes to lower me and brought me to the ground. After cleaning the anchor and salvaging what gear he could, he joined me at the base of the cliff. Here, we assessed our options for an evacuation. Our choices included calling for a rescue, bushwhacking to the river and hitting a gravel road, or ascending the approach gully and then hiking back to the car. We chose to ascend the gully because I was able to walk and we didn't want to bushwhack in the dark. The approach gully includes two fifth class sections. We made it to the first fifth-class section, an overhanging rock of approximately 20 feet in height. Nathan ascended the single fixed rope. At the top he built an anchor and rigged a 3:1 to haul me up the rock. About two-thirds of the way up the rock, two of the three anchor points blew and I slammed into the rock. I don't believe this caused any further injury, but it sure hurt like hell!

The second fifth class section went without incident. We hiked the remaining section of trail back to the car. The evacuation, from accident to vehicle, had taken approximately five hours. We drove to Mission Hospital in Asheville, where I was treated for a badly broken collarbone and a broken scapula, as well as a laceration on the elbow to the bone, a hematoma on the hip, bruised ribs, sternum, elbow, and ankle, and torn ligaments in the rotator cuff. The elbow and the hip were suspected to be fractured but x-rays proved negative. After follow-up assessment, the collarbone required reconstructive surgery with "bone putty", seven screws, and a six-inch titanium plate. As of September 1st, I am still in physical therapy, but returned to the rock two weeks ago—the first time since my accident.

## Analysis

In hindsight, there were a number of things we could have done which may have prevented this accident. First, we should have been satisfied after climbing Maginot Line, and not starting a multi-pitch climb at 4:30 p.m. in January. Fatigue should have been a warning sign, suggesting to us that it would have been best to descend after completing the first pitch. When I realized I was off route and run out, I could have exercised caution and down-climbed, or I could have consulted more than one guidebook for route information, placed more protection, or stayed home and watched football! (Source: John Matthew)

Additional Comment: Linville Gorge is a remote area with very challenging terrain and access. Rescue is often difficult and demanding in time, manpower, and equipment. Both climbers did an excellent job of being self-sufficient and skilled in initiating a self-rescue. (Source: Aram Attarian)

## SLIP ON ROCK – FAILURE TO TEST HOLDS, CAM PULLED OUT, PLACED INADEQUATE PROTECTION, EXCEEDING ABILITIES
### North Carolina, Jackson County, Gray's Ridge

Chris Wilcox (35) and Scott Philyaw (52), both experienced climbers, had busy home and work lives that prevented them from getting out more than once a month at best, with rather longer periods of inactivity during winter ski season and summer rains. Scott also had some wilderness medicine training in his background. Chris describes their misadventure as follows:

Neither of us had experience in establishing new routes, but over the previous year, we were increasingly drawn by the lure of exploring some un-touched rock faces in eastern Jackson County. One cliff in particular caught our fancy, so in the second half of 2007, we twice scouted Gray's Ridge, which forms the high, northwest side of Wolf Creek Gorge in the Little Canada section of Jackson County. At its highest, the southeast-facing cliff is about 450 feet, broken by at least one major, wooded ramp. The approach is a strenuous bushwhack and there were no visible signs that it had ever been climbed. Finally on March 9th, we got a late start and made the roughly one hour approach on National Forest land, across a steep, choked tributary to Wolf Creek, then up and to the southwest to a likely looking jumping off point by approximately 1330.

Scott offered me the honor of first lead, which I to accepted. I opted to leave my new bolt kit on the ground as the possibilities for protection on the first pitch looked good. I headed up on solid but dirty 5.6-5.7 terrain and placed a couple of secure cams roughly ten and 15 feet off the ground. The climbing for the next 40 feet remained easy on solid-seeming rock that gradually got more thickly covered with lichen as the angle rolled off to a ledge where I intended to belay. My two pieces of protection in this interval were small cams (the last, I think, was a 0.5 Trango cam), but they were the only placements I could find and were in two short, flaring, downward facing cracks, maybe 25 and 35 feet off the ground.

Despite sensing that the last piece was just "psycho-pro," I moved up another five to ten feet onto lichen-covered footholds as the angle of the rock face slackened. I over-committed to one of these untested footholds and it popped off. I slid, pulling out my top two placements. My right leg struck the ledge that made the stance for the first pieces of protection and I flipped end-over-end, striking my helmet. I believe the top two pieces of protection (which failed), and the strike on the ledge absorbed some of the energy of what amounted to a fifty-foot slide/tumble.

When I came to a stop maybe ten feet down the steep slope from the base of the rock, Scott was below me urging me not to move. My only obvious and serious injury was an open tib/fib fracture. A self-evacuation was out of the question. My injury, coupled with the late hour and the steep/choked nature of the surrounding terrain, necessitated a technical rescue involving outside resources.

We tried several times to get a cell phone signal with no luck. Before Scott hiked out to summon help, he applied traction and supported my leg as I moved in a crab walk to a more level spot and on top of a rope tarp. He used my plastic latrine trowel and gauze and cling wrap to improvise a splint. Scott then made sure I had put on all our spare outer-layers including a stocking cap under my helmet. I loaded up on Ibuprofen and settled in to feed, hydrate, and watch the clock. Scott left me at 1510. By 1545, he had retraced our approach, flagged down a passing motorist, and caught a ride to a house to place a call to 911.

Members of the Little Canada Fire Department were familiar with the terrain and responded within a short time, meeting Scott back at the trailhead to where he had returned. The whistle I keep in my shell helped the first member of the Jackson County Rescue Squad on rappel to find me quickly. The incident commander sent another squad member and a paramedic down the same line. Rescuers outlined the options being planned above. Although the Rescue Squad was trained and equipped for a haul up the cliff, complex terrain with loose rock and interspersed with heavy vegetation combined with the late hour caused the incident commander to request the aid of a helicopter.

At 1810 the heli-team was overhead, performing a recon/assessment. Two team members lowered through the forest canopy and directed the ground-based rescuers in packaging me for hoist and transport. By 1845 I was transferred into a ground ambulance at the Jackson County Airport. In the final assessment my injuries included a highly comminuted pilon fracture of the tibia, an open fibular fracture, a cracked calcaneous, and chipped patella. I sprained the medial and lateral cruciate ligaments and scuffed the meniscus in my right knee.

**Analysis**

While the technical difficulty of the rock I encountered was within my ability, I should probably have pushed up through the grades a bit more before turning my attention to unexplored rock. I would also have benefited from more frequent repetition of my leading skills. My complete lack of experience in establishing new routes also contributed to the length of my fall. I did not clean the features in which I placed protection and I left our bolt kit on the ground.

Probable factors in this latter decision include unfamiliarity with use of the hand-drill, and a reluctance to place bolts from stances near what "looked like" good natural protection. In retrospect, I should have down-climbed and retrieved the bolt kit. Also, I could have prevented the fall by being more methodical in testing my foot placements before committing full weight to them. (Source: Scott Philyaw)

## FALL OR SLIP ON ROCK, INADEQUATE BELAY, INEXPERIENCED
### North Carolina, Looking Glass Rock

On May 8, a male climber (31) and his female partner were attempting an unknown rock climb when he fell and broke his ankle. It was broken on both sides and will need surgery, plates, screws, and pins, to put it back together. Other climbers in the area assisted him to the trailhead.

No one on the scene is sure why he fell, but the evidence suggests that he was new to the area and got himself in over his head. His girlfriend was belaying with a GriGri, but was not a climber herself. Climbers near the scene reported he was climbing on eyebrows above a crack on a 5.6 single pitch route, possibly "Good Intentions", when they heard him yell, "Take!" His girlfriend yelled back, "Don't fall, wait!" He yelled back that his hands were too slick and he couldn't hold on any longer and to "take" and get ready for the fall. She yelled back, "Please, no, wait!"

When he fell it looked like his last piece was at his feet and he was squatting before bailing off and taking a 20-foot fall. By the time he was caught, he swung into a big bulge and immediately broke his ankle.

Witnesses reported that it appeared that his belayer had a significant amount of time to take up the slack but didn't know how to take in slack quickly on a GriGri.

### Analysis

Moral of the story: belaying is a climbing skill that should not be taken lightly, familiarize yourself (and your significant other) with your chosen belay device! Down-climbing is an important basic climbing skill that every climber should embrace. (Source: From a post on carolinaclimbers.org, May 9).

### FALL ON ROCK, INAPPROPRIATE CALL TO 911
### North Carolina, Rumbling Bald, Drivin and Cryin

On May 21, while preparing to climb, an EMS vehicle entered the Rumbling Bald parking lot. One of the EMT's asked if anyone had called 911, noting that someone had called saying they had fallen "below the cliff". Without further conversation, he left the parking lot. Shortly thereafter, other rescue personnel began to arrive, including two state park rangers, assorted volunteer firemen, paramedics, and rescue vehicles!

My partner and I left the lot and hiked to the climb Gunboat Diplomacy. Upon arriving, we heard someone yelling. I walked over to investigate and found a climber sitting below Drivin and Cryin (5.10a) with an obviously swollen ankle but otherwise okay. He stated that he fell above the first bolt (bolt was clipped) and broke his ankle. I followed by telling him that a group of rescue personnel were on their way.

Shortly thereafter, a group of approximately ten rescuers arrived. The climber was assessed for injuries and after some consultation, he walked out under his own power with minimal assistance.

### Analysis

Climbers have a responsibility to attempt a self-rescue and that calling 911 should be the very, very last option. Climbers should take personal responsibility for being in the mountains and climbing safely. By adopting skills and gaining the appropriate knowledge, training, and experience, climbers can reduce risks to acceptable limits. More rescues, especially unnecessary ones performed by local and government agencies, have the potential to impact the climbing community negatively. (Source: Will Byrum from a posting on carolinaclimbers.org, May 22, and Aram Attarian)

## FATIGUE, FALL ON ROCK, EXCEEDING ABILITIES
### North Carolina, Hanging Rock State Park — Moores Wall, Dolphin Head

On May 25, Chris Hagwood (42) and Mark Ericson (52), experienced climbers, started Dolphin Head (5.6), a popular rock climb located on Moores' Central Wall, and shortly went off-route. Before he knew it, Chris was in over his head. Instead of continuing, he had Mark lower him to the ground. Mark said he felt sure he could finish the route instead of leaving some of Chris' gear behind. A third climber had recently bailed on another nearby route and this compounded the pair's frustration at leaving routes unfinished.

Mark successfully led the first pitch to a belay anchor just under the dolphin head feature of the climb. Chris followed to the belay. Mark started the second pitch and placed a cam to the right of the feature as he attempted to pull over it. He successfully stepped back down to the belay after one or more failed attempts. On two subsequent attempts to get over the feature, he fell trying to step back down to the belay. On the first two falls, he recovered and tried again after a few minutes. While trying to pull over the feature for a third time, he hooked his foot on the feature in such a way that when he fell, his foot over-rotated and he fractured his ankle at the base of the tibia.

Chris was able to lower Mark from the belay to the ground, where a third climber assisted. During the lower, the rope got tangled around a "chicken head." Chris was able to keep Mark locked off and loosen the rope until it was freed. After being lowered to the ground, Chris rappelled from the belay anchor and pulled the rope.

Mark was able to stand, but could not walk, so he mostly "scooted" down the trail. The party called for assistance with their cell phone from North Carolina State Park Rangers, since the trail was too narrow for assisted walking. A pick-up truck reached the climbers at the upper-most area that could accommodate a vehicle. Mark was transported in the bed of the truck while Chris and the third climber were driven back to the climber's parking lot by the rangers. Unsure of the condition of his ankle (but suspecting a moderate to severe sprain), Mark was driven home. A visit to his doctor the next day revealed the broken ankle.

## Analysis

We were both tired from a day of climbing. Chris was attempting a route above his ability. We should have left the stopper in place that Chris originally lowered from and walked away. Alternately, we should have converted the belay anchor into a rappel anchor and lowered off after falling the first time on the feature We should not have attempted to press on. (Source: Chris Hagwood and Mark Erickson)

## INADEQUATE PROTECTION – NUT PULLED OUT, FALL ON ROCK, NO HARD HAT
### North Carolina, Looking Glass Rock, Second Coming

On July 28, at 9:00 p.m. two climbers called 911 from the base of Second Coming, a well-known 5.7 two pitch traditional climb located on the Southside of Looking Glass Rock.

Jane Doe was belaying John Doe (31) on the first pitch of Second Coming. John was leading the first pitch and was about 100 feet off the ground at the 5.7 crux, where he placed a stopper. After a few unsuccessful attempts at the crux, John was lowered to the ground through the *single stopper* placement.

Jane Doe decided to give the climb a try and began to top-rope on the single stopper placed earlier by John. She was able to work her way through the crux and ignored a good ledge and the standard belay for the route. Instead she climbed past a large flake and continued up the second pitch of the climb, reaching the double crack system.

There are two crack systems on the second pitch: one diminishes while the other begins about 15 to 20 feet to the right of the first. Jane could not find her way up the first crack and did not see the second crack to the right. (This would be the easiest way to the top of the second pitch).

Jane placed then lowered off a blue tri-cam. John lowered her to the large flake about 20 feet below the tri-cam placement, where she was able to build a three-point anchor using passive pro in the flake. Once the anchor was built, Jane brought John up to her position, belaying him from her harness with a re-direct through the anchor.

Once John arrived and clipped into the anchor, he lowered Jane off his belay device attached to his harness with the rope re-directed through the anchor. Once Jane had been lowered approximately 120 feet to the ground, John began building a rappel anchor by repositioning it a little higher in the flake. (He thought that the rock was a bit hollow where Jane had positioned it earlier). John placed a stopper in the crack as the primary anchor point. This placement was backed up with a second stopper on a sling. The two pieces were placed close together with room between them (not equalized). Once the anchor was built, John placed himself on rappel.

Somewhere between the start of his rappel and approximately 100 feet from the ground, the top stopper failed. The rest is speculation, but it is believed that the force of the top stopper failing and the bottom catching created a shock-load that caused the second stopper to fail. At this point, Jane stated that she heard John scream. She looked to see John falling from 100 feet above! John hit a ledge about 30 feet below the crux and tumbled down the slab below.

Brevard Rescue Squad responded to Jane's 911 call and evacuated John via litter and backboard. He sustained lacerations to the top of his head, a broken shoulder blade, a severe contusion on his elbow, a broken wrist (requiring surgery), and a bruised hip. John was not wearing a helmet. He was transported to Mission Hospitals in Asheville, NC.

## Analysis

A couple of potentially dangerous scenarios were evident in this event. First, John was lowered through a single nut placement, then Jane chose to top-rope through that same single nut rather than pull the rope and re-lead the pitch. These actions are a high-risk maneuver given that a single stopper protects the climbing 100 feet off the deck! While it didn't contribute at all to the accident, it in itself could be considered a near miss.

Second, by placing all of the anchor points behind a flake they were literally "placing all of their eggs in one basket." A common test to determine the integrity of a flake is to strike it. If it sounds hollow avoid it. Flakes are known to expand. This is especially true when using passive protection like stoppers. The wedging action of the stoppers more than likely caused the flake to expand, causing the anchor to fail. Safer options may have included abandoning the climb once John was on the ground, rappel off an *equalized anchor*, or to continue up easier terrain to the Gemini Cracks rappel anchors. As always a helmet is recommended! (Source: Edited from a post on carolinaclimbers.org and Aram Attarian.)

## FALL ON SNOW, CLIMBING UNROPED
### Oregon, Mount Hood, Southside

On July 5, Erik Heerlein (35), a climber from South Carolina, fell approximately 200 feet while descending the Mazama Chute variation (10,500-foot elevation) of the Southside Route. His unroped team members included an M.D. and a paramedic. They were able to report the accident via cellphone and provide emergency medical aid. Heerlein struck his head (some protection was provided by a bicycle helmet) and lost consciousness during the fall. He was transported to a local hospital by a Blackhawk helicopter.

## Analysis

Although this route is often climbed unroped during normal conditions, the exposure provides ample opportunity for injury during a fall. The security provided by the rope should always be considered. The helmet likely minimized the head injury. Having an M.D. and paramedic in one's party is always good fortune. (Source: Jeff Sheetz, Portland Mountain Rescue)

## FALLING ROCK, WEATHER, LATE START
### Oregon, Mount Hood, Cooper Spur

On July 27, Dr. Gary Lee (55), an experienced climber, and his son Devin (20) finished the ascent of the Sunshine route in the early afternoon. They descended by the Cooper Spur route, stopping at a snowfield at the 10,000-foot level to unrope and don crampons. Believing that the worst part of the climb was behind them, they continued down the snowfield until a watermelon-sized rock struck Dr. Lee in the back and sent him tumbling down the fall line. He fell about 1000 feet out of sight and became wedged between boulders on the steep north face. Devon continued descending, calling after his father, but was unable to make contact. He was met by two hikers who placed a 911-cell phone call notifying authorities of the accident.

The body recovery by ground teams involved hazards associated with loose rock on the exposed north face and included an airdrop of a 600-foot rope.

### Analysis

Nearby climbers observed the pair during their ascent and noted their lateness on route. Also, the previous night remained warm, so the snow surface did not freeze/stabilize. Climbers must adjust their schedules for early starts to beat the diurnal heating cycle and be well clear of rockfall hazards by mid-morning. Rescuers experienced late season conditions (thin snowcover, icy surfaces, and excessive rockfall). The party's upper descent route was completely free of snow/ice, thereby exposing a bed of unstable rock. Though the party did not wear helmets, this choice would probably not have affected the outcome of such a long fall. However, this might be an indicator of their unawareness of the climbing conditions. (Source: Jeff Sheetz, Portland Mountain Rescue)

## FALL ON SNOW, UNABLE TO SELF-ARREST, CLIMBING ALONE, EXCEEDING ABILITIES
### Oregon, Mount Hood, Southside

On October 19, Chris Biddle (30), a novice climber, lost his footing at 10,900-foot elevation while descending the Southside Route. Unable to self-arrest he slid about 300 feet. A nearby climber who witnessed the fall reported his accident via cell phone. The witness and another climber were able to stabilize Biddle until a PMR ground team (supplemented by AMR Reach-and-Treat medics) climbed to the accident sites. The subject was air-evacuated by a Blackhawk helicopter to a local hospital.

## Analysis
Late season conditions (normal in October!) existed on the route making the novice climb technically difficult. Biddle later admitted that he had gone beyond his abilities to travel safely on the icy terrain. Without the support of a rope team, a novice solo climber takes great risks on technical terrain. (Source: Jeff Sheetz, Portland Mountain Rescue)

## FALL ON ICE, ROPE SEVERED ON JAGGED ROCKS
### Pennsylvania, Toby Creek, Buttermilk Falls
Police in Luzerne County say Luke Wolfgang (age not reported) fell 30-40 feet when his rope was cut on jagged rocks as he tried to climb the Buttermilk Falls area of Toby Creek.

Rescuers say the New Hope man was climbing with friends yesterday morning when the accident occurred. They say he was taken to a Scranton hospital with injuries that did not appear life-threatening, though he did suffer some broken bones.

Officials say his friends had to walk to the highway to get help because there is no cell phone service in the climbing area. (Source: From an Associated Press article sent to us with no date or additional information.)

## FALL ON ROCK, CLIMBING UNROPED
### Pennsylvania, Tohickon Valley Park
Joseph McDevitt (26) was in serious condition yesterday after plunging at least 70 feet to the ground in a fall off a cliff in Bucks County. He was airlifted and treated in the intensive care unit at St. Luke's Hospital near Bethlehem, officials said.

### Analysis
The 200-foot cliffs of red shale along Tohickon Creek are popular among climbers. While falls like McDevitt's "do occur, it's not commonplace," county spokesman Chris Edwards said.

A witness said McDevitt had no rope or safety harness. Witnesses differed on whether McDevitt wore a helmet. (Source, from an article by Jeff Gammage, in the *Philadelphia Inquirer.* No date given)

*(Editor's Note: We are sure that other incidents occur in PA. At the moment, we rely on inconsistent sources for information from this region.)*

## FALL ON ROCK – RAPPEL ERROR (UNEVEN ROPES)
### South Dakota, Needles, Moonlight Ridge
Another climbing legend passed on today. On June 24, Paul Duval (71) died of injuries sustained when he rappelled off the end of an un-equalized rope at Moonlight Ridge.

Paul was a very humble and gentle man. His contributions to rock climbing were numerous. We will miss him.

## Analysis

Paul had set up a rappel using someone else's rope that had multiple markings, including markings about 20 feet from each end. Paul was not familiar with this latest in rope-design. It appears that he short-roped one side due the selection of the wrong rope marking, which he apparently assumed was the middle mark. He had passed the first marking on the rope and then went all the way to the next mark, which was actually an end 'alert' mark, about 20 feet from the end of the rope. The center mark was faded and difficult to see. The short end of the rope was over a small overhang and Paul was facing in the opposite direction looking over an adjacent route off his left side. The overhang and short rope were off to his right side. He was also talking to the people who were on the ground and farther around toward the opposite side of the rock. Neither Paul nor the people on the ground ever saw or noticed that there was a short rope side to the rappel set-up and a very long side, because both ends were around a corner and behind Paul to his right. (Source: Peter Lev)

*(Editor's Note: There are ways to ensure one has found the middle of the rope. The old fashioned way, guaranteed to work, is to grab both ends and slide back until reaching the bight of rope, which is the middle. Another method is to knot the ends of the rappel rope together so that it will jam in the rappel device.*

*Another reason the middle mark can be wrong is if one of the ends was cut off due to damage or some other reason.)*


## FALL ON ROCK
### Utah, Zion National Park, Moonlight Buttress

Early on the afternoon of March 24th, a climber (40) who was following the first pitch of the Moonlight Buttress took an unexpectedly long pendulum swing, struck the rock wall, and sustained an incapacitating hip injury. One of his partners descended and reported the accident to a shuttle bus driver. Rangers responded and reached the injured man via a short technical climb to the small ledge he was resting on, which was about 50 feet above the talus slope at the base of the route. He was packaged and lowered via a guiding line system to a waiting litter team that carried him down the scree slope and across the Virgin River to a waiting park ambulance.

Doctors diagnosed his injury as a fractured pelvis. The rescue involved 14 park staffers and was completed during daylight hours. Ranger Andrew Fitzgerald was the operations supervisor. (Source from a report by Bonnie Schwartz, Chief Ranger, Zion National Park)

## FALL ON ROCK – RAPPEL ERROR
### Utah, Big cottonwood Canyon

On May 5, a man (22) rappelling in Big Cottonwood Canyon survived a fall of more than 50 feet. He was rappelling with friends near Storm Mountain around 4:00 p.m. He suffered a broken leg and was flown to University Hospital in serious condition.

### Analysis

"He was using a two-rope system but didn't attach the second rope," said Salt Lake County Sheriff's Lt. Paul Jaroscak. "He got to the end of the first rope and went into a free-fall." (Source: From a posting on mountainproject.com)

*(Editor's Note: We are still finding this kind of incident. The assumption here is that the man and his friend were part of a contingent that merely likes to go rappelling.)*

## FALL ON ROCK, PROTECTION PULLED OUT, INADEQUATE PROTECTION, EXCEEDING ABILITIES, NO HARD HAT
### Utah, Indian Creek, Cat Wall

On May 17, a man and his wife and their two friends (ages unknown) were climbing Johnny Cat (5.12+). The man was going for the final moves, just below the anchor, when he fell. His last piece failed with the force, and due to his sparse protection, allowed him to deck. He hit head first, no helmet, recoiled with the rope, and crashed violently on his right shoulder. His vitals were a rollercoaster and the depth of his injuries unclear.

About 30 minutes later, the park service arrived. They brought more advanced first aid, which greatly helped, and let the IC situation stay as is while they coordinated other resources including Flight for Life and SAR. It was another 30-plus minutes after that that Paramedics, the rescue equipment, and SAR arrived. Once on scene, they took command. We all continued to work together, getting the victim fully stabilized and ready for transport. Then, in one co-operative effort, we took him successfully down the hillside.

Once down, the pros stabilized him and drained some internal fluids to get him ready for the flight. They then flew him and his wife to Grand Junction.

### Analysis

Follow gear recommendations in guide and protection standards of type of climbing. In this case, one placement for at least every body length, don't push beyond limits without proper protection, wear your helmet, and be prepared for any and all possible emergencies when climbing in the backcountry or severe isolation. (Source: From a posting by Shane Neal)

## FALL ON ROCK, INADEQUATE BELAY — UNFAMILIAR WITH BELAY DEVICE
### Utah, Maple Canyon, Minimum Crag

On July 13, Paul R. (47) fell 50 to 60 feet while climbing "49" at the Minimum Crag. His belayer was using an Edelrid Eddy. He was using a 9.2mm rope, which falls within the manufacturers recommended rope diameters. The belayer claims that the climber was clipping a draw when he fell; the climber claims he was not clipping a draw at the time of the fall. Irrelevant, but part of the situation. From what I have been able to surmise, the belayer felt the rope tug, depressed the device "trigger" and tossed out what he thought would be an armload of rope. This is why it resulted in a 50-foot fall.

### Analysis

A review of the device description states, "The design makes it impossible to hold the cam open in this way—it's simply not big enough to hold [during a fall]." The belayer states that he was not holding the climber side of the rope during the fall. By holding the climber side of the rope exiting the device, it would render the device useless. (Source: From a posting by "maddog" on mountainproject.com)

Another point of view by Mark Horan, who got this review from *Rock & Ice*:

The Eddy is no Grigri, and it costs twice as much. Need to read more? OK: The Eddy, Edelrid's new auto-locking device, intends to improve on what could be perceived as Grigri "weaknesses"—those being the danger of holding the lever open or not clipping the two side plates together.

Admittedly, there are definite safety improvements with the Eddy. First, the two side plates lock into place with a click, eliminating the chance of only clipping through one side plate. And unlike the Grigri, which relies on rope friction to engage a cam to hold the rope in place, the Eddy uses rope friction to engage a cam that locks into place. I can see how these features improve safety, however, the Eddy snagged up all tasks, from lowering to feeding line. I experimented with holding the Eddy in different hand positions, but the device inevitably and invariably locked up, leaving me scrambling to figure out how to unlock the cam (press it down and it will release) to continue feeding slack.

The Eddy, a rather heavy bugger at 12.4 ounces (Grigri is 7.9 ounces), will also lock if the user pulls the lever all the way back. This eliminates the risk of the belayer dropping you because he freaked and yarded on the lever. I found this feature especially annoying and even superfluous to safety. First, it makes the lever's range of arc that unlocks the cam extremely small so that you have to pull it back just right in order to lower your partner.

To sum up, the Eddy is okay. It will catch and lower any climber—even on, thank god, ropes down to 9 millimeters! However, compared to the no nonsense Grigri, I found the Eddy difficult to use.

## FALL ON ROCK, ASCENDERS ATTACHED INCORRECTLY — ROPE SEVERED
### Utah, Zion National Park, Touchstone Wall

Shortly after 2:00 p.m. on October 17th, James Welton (34), Matt Tuttle, and I started up Touchstone Wall (III 5.9+ C2 1,000 feet). Though we considered trying to climb the route in a day, we decided to spend one night on the wall. We reasoned that this would allow us to be more relaxed during our climb. Additionally, starting in the afternoon would let us stay out of the way of any faster parties that began the route in the morning. All three of us were looking forward to spending the night high above the ground in a spectacular setting.

Matt led the first pitch, James led the slightly overhanging second pitch, and I led the third. The leader climbed on a 70m x 9.1mm Beal Joker dynamic rope, and trailed a 70m x 10mm static haul-line. Upon completion of each pitch, the leader then fixed, or anchored, both ropes to permanent drilled anchors. The two followers then used mechanical ascenders to simultaneously climb the two ropes. We had one set of Black Diamond nForce ascenders and one set of Petzl Ascensions. All four ascenders were in excellent condition. At the time of the accident, James was using the Petzl ascenders.

At the top of the third pitch, we determined that our haul line was long enough to reach the top of the fourth pitch without hauling. We decided to make one long haul rather than two shorter hauls. Matt led the fourth pitch mostly free. While Matt climbed, James and I reveled in the beauty of Zion Canyon and agreed that we were having a wonderful time.

When Matt reached the anchor, he fixed both ropes and attached a Petzl Pro Traxion and swivel to the static rope in preparation for hauling. James and I then lowered out the haul bag so that it was hanging from the anchors at the top of the fourth pitch. James prepared to ascend the haul line while I readied myself to climb the lead line and clean the pitch.

The fall occurred at dusk (shortly after 7:00 p.m.) for reasons that are unclear.

When James fell, I looked up from the anchor and witnessed him falling, quickly and upright, along the rope. Apparently, his ascenders initially provided little or no resistance to the fall. After falling a significant distance, James jerked violently and fell the rest of the way to the ground—a total of 200 feet.

James' fall was mercifully quick and every indication suggests that he died on impact. Two nearby climbers responded to my calls for help and were at the base of the route in minutes. Matt and I returned to the ground safely, albeit slowly. The dark rappels were interminable. Emergency personnel were on the scene by the time we reached the ground.

## Analysis

Post-accident investigation of the equipment and the rope indicates that James fell between 20 and 40 feet before his ascenders engaged the rope. When his ascenders did engage, the force of the fall caused the ascenders to sever the static rope's sheath and, shortly thereafter, the core. On the ground, one of James' ascenders was found still attached to the rope, about a foot below the break. There was significant bunching of the rope's sheath above and below this ascender. The other ascender was found nearby. Both devices were still attached to James' harness and daisy chain. No significant rope damage was found above the break, which was located about 60 feet from the haulbag at the end of the rope.

According to Petzl's specifications for the Ascension, rope damage or failure can occur under loads in the range of 5–6 kN. James' fall would have generated a load upwards of 10 kN.

It was dusk, though we were in no particular danger or difficulty, and it was still light out when James fell. Later analysis of our position suggests that we were not as far on the route as we initially thought, because there are multiple anchors in the middle of some of the pitches on Touchstone. It's possible that James was in a hurry, and did not pay close attention to his set-up. Additionally, James primarily used Black Diamond ascenders, which have a slightly different trigger mechanism than the Petzl ascenders he was using when he fell. It is possible that this minor equipment difference contributed to the fall. Also, James was not using a Grigri to back up his ascenders. All three of us had used Grigri backups until this point. However, since the static line was under load, using a Grigri to back up the ascenders would have been impossible. A prusik or autoblock back-up probably would have saved James' life. Also, ascending a loaded rope can introduce difficulties.

James apparently failed to correctly attach his ascenders to the rope he was preparing to ascend. It is not clear how he was under the impression that his ascenders were correctly engaged or how he removed himself from the anchor without first weighting his ascenders. After unclipping from the anchor, he fell about 30 feet along the rope, at which time his ascenders engaged the rope. The ascenders, in the process of catching the fall, damaged the rope to the point of failure.

Upon reaching the high point of the climb, Matt Tuttle attached the haul rope to the anchor and then affixed a Petzl Pro Traxion to the haul rope. There was about 15 feet of slack between the Pro Traxion and the end of that rope, which was fixed to the anchor. Apparently, it is possible to attach a Traxion in such a way that it appears to be correctly engaged and that it will hold SOME weight, but in fact it will not. When James added his weight to the haul rope and began to ascend, the rope slid through the Pro

Traxion and came tight on the anchor. This 15-foot static fall was sufficient to cause James' ascenders to sever his rope. (Source: Perry Hooker)

## FALL INTO CREVASSE
### Washington, Mount Rainier, enroute to Wilson Headwall

On the morning of May 4th, three climbers left Camp Muir, following a gentle downhill traverse to reach the base of the Wilson Headwall. About ten minutes out from the camp, they stopped to scout and evaluate the need for roping up prior to entering a known crevasse area. While stopped, one of the climbers fell through the snow into a crevasse to a depth of approximately 120 feet. The climbers were able to put out a distress radio call via the park frequency. Climbing ranger Arlington Ashby responded within 15 minutes of the call from Camp Muir and assessed the situation. Climbing rangers Thomas Payne and Joe Franklin soon arrived from Camp Muir to assist in the rescue, with Payne assuming the role as team lead. The stranded climber was wedged head-first deep in the crevasse, giving responders only two feet of vertical space in which to maneuver. After removing his pack by cutting the straps, they were able to haul him out of the crevasse.

"The position of the climber, stranded headfirst at a very narrow point in the crevasse, combined with his hypothermic condition, made time a critical issue and a quick crevasse rescue imperative," said incident commander David Gottlieb. Due to these factors, the climber was removed from the crevasse, placed on a backboard, and then taken to Camp Muir. A Bell Jet Ranger helicopter was placed on standby to fly him out once the weather cleared. During this time, rangers worked with the Northwest Helicopters pilot to reconfigure the Jet Ranger to carry a litter. Although the climber fell a long distance, he suffered only superficial wounds. (Source: Patti Wold, Incident Information Officer)

## PARTY SEPARATED ON SUMMIT – WHITEOUT
### Washington, Mount Rainier

On May 4th, two climbers left Paradise at 9:00 p.m. with the intention of doing a single-push summit climb and skiing back down the mountain via Fuhrers Thumb. In the afternoon, the park received a 911 call from one of the climbers reporting that he'd become separated from his partner and lost in a whiteout somewhere on the summit.

That evening, his partner skied down to Paradise. On Tuesday morning, the park brought in a Hughes 500 helicopter operated by Whirlwind Helicopters and organized a two-person observation team. A break in the weather permitted the observation flight around mid-day, during which the observers located the climber on the summit. The helicopter was found to be too heavy to take on another passenger at 14,000+ feet, so the pilot returned to the Kautz Heli-base to drop off one of the rangers. During the observation flight, the pilot exceeded the aircraft's capabilities, causing it to overheat. The climber eventually tired of waiting for the helicopter to return and skied down to Paradise. There were no injuries or accidents due to the overheating of the aircraft. Said Gottlieb, who was also IC for the second incident: "It is our responsibility to respond to requests for assistance proactively; a delayed response costs lives here." (Source: Patti Wold, Incident Information Officer)

*(Editor's Note: While this is not counted as an accident, it illustrates a potential for a problem when cell phones are used and helicopters are brought into play. It is also interesting to note that the climber who apparently was not lost in the whiteout decided to ski to the base without his partner.)*

## WEATHER – STRANDED
### Washington, Mount Rainier

Two climbers, Mrs. Mariana Burceag and Mr. Daniel Vlad (ages unknown), suffering from hypothermia and frostbite, were airlifted from Camp Muir on Mount Rainier at 6:15 a.m. on June 18 by a Chinook helicopter. They were taken to Madigan Hospital and from there by ground transportation to Harborview Medical Center in Seattle. Mr. Eduard Burceag (age unknown), the husband of Mrs. Burceag, died of injuries sustained in the incident. His body is being removed from mountain this afternoon.

The three individuals are experienced mountaineers who had visited Camp Muir in the past and have enjoyed hiking and climbing on Mount Rainier for many years. Two had previously reached the summit. On June 16, they became trapped on the Muir Snowfield by a sudden blizzard while descending from a day hike to Camp Muir. Early on June 17, a 911 emergency call came through to park rangers advising them of overdue climbers on the Muir Snowfield. Due to heavy, drifting snow, 70 mph winds, and near zero visibility, a rescue team was unable to initiate a search safely at that time. At 7:15 a.m., one member of the party found his way to Camp Muir and was able to direct a search team, made up of climbing guides and park rangers stationed at Camp Muir, to the party's location near Anvil Rock. All three were under shelter by 8:30 a.m. Three doctors who were at Camp Muir as clients of one of the park's guide services provided immediate medical care. Mr. Burceag was unconscious and unresponsive upon arrival. Rescuers were unable to revive him.

The shelter at Camp Muir is warm, dry, and well-stocked with food and water. A carry-out rescue could have been initiated following the rescue; however, rangers and doctors determined it would be in the best interest of the patients to spend the night and wait for a break in the weather to safely fly the next day. This morning dawned clear above Camp Muir, with heavy clouds below. The Chinook helicopter arrived at 6:00 a.m. and in approximately 15 minutes, lifted Mrs. Burceag and Mr. Vlad, along with one of the park's climbing rangers, into the helicopter by hoist and cable. Those on scene report that the cloud ceiling had risen somewhat by the time the helicopter arrived and that the rescue occurred amid swirling clouds that threatened to engulf the mountain in fog.

## Analysis

Every year, roughly 9,000 people climb Mount Rainier and only about half of them reach the summit. Thousands more take day hikes or overnight camping trips to Camp Muir (48 were registered there on that night). These individuals are attracted by the majesty of the mountain, the wilderness experience, and the breathtaking beauty of mornings like this one, high above the clouds on the side of the volcano. Like many things in life, there are inherent risks in the wilderness. Sudden storms like Monday's blizzard can catch even the most experienced and prepared hikers off guard. Visitors should check in with park rangers for the latest information about conditions on the mountain and should always be prepared for an emergency. (Source: Edited from a report on the mountrainierclimbing.blogspot.com)

## FALL ON ROCK – SCRAMBLING WITH FULL PACK, WEATHER and FALL OFF LOG – STREAM CROSSING
### Washington, North Cascades National Perk, Inspiration Traverse

On July 26, Cathleen (50) and Bob Terczak (50's) were on day four of an alpine traverse across the southern section of the park known as the Inspiration Traverse. This traverse involves route-finding from heavily wooded valley floors to subalpine ridges and on to significant glacier crossings. Mountaineers often include numerous peak ascents along the traverse. While the trip can be made without significant technical climbing, glacier experience is necessary and conditions and terrain warrant the ability to negotiate steep forest and rock sections with a full pack.

The Terczaks spent the night of the 25th bivied on the summit of Primus Peak. On the 26th they hoped to make a camp on the eastern Inspiration Glacier, after crossing sections of three other glaciers first (North Klawatti, Klawatti, and McAllister). Near the end of the day, the pair reached the col that separates the Klawatti and McAllister Glaciers, which involves an approximate 150-foot ascent over rock. Complications included deteriorating weather (wind and fog moving in) and a significant mote on their side of the col. Both climbers scrambled up carrying heavy packs and checking for a route over when Cathleen fell approximately 35 feet from a ledge into a moat separating glacier ice from a rock wall. Bob descended, moved Cathleen from the moat down the glacier to a point he could erect their tent. He cared for her for 24 hours, unable to reach a cell connection, before she died in their tent. (Later medical report indicated head injury as cause of death.) Bob then crossed three glaciers and over several off-trail miles, descending 6000 feet. Just before reaching a road, he fell from a log while crossing a river, nearly drowned and injured one knee, before jettisoning his pack and getting unpinned. Other climbers found him on the road and delivered him to the NPS ranger station during the night.

Continuous fog had replaced the earlier good weather after the Terczak's accident. During the day Bob traveled out, a NOLS group traveled this section of the traverse in the opposite direction, finding the oddly placed tent along their way. The NOLS leader used a satellite phone to call the NPS dispatch and reported a deceased woman at their location. Rangers began to prepare for the recovery and to find the partner prior to his making it out.

Attempts to reach the accident site by helicopter were thwarted for two full days due to poor weather. During a window of clear weather between two storms, rangers recovered the deceased climber's body from the top of the Klawatti Glacier.

**Analysis**

This couple from Delaware had been spending mountaineering vacations in the North Cascades for many years, having accomplished other alpine traverses and technical peak ascents. They were well equipped with appropriate gear and Cathleen was wearing a helmet during the scramble and across the glaciers. Her husband did not see the actual fall despite being nearby, approximately ten feet below her, when she fell. The two had actually just decided to down-climb and retreat back to the Klawatti Glacier due to the deteriorating weather and it being unclear if the route over the col was a "go". It is not known what exactly led to her falling.

This particular col is traveled relatively often by mountaineers attempting the Inspiration Traverse or climbing peaks in the area. Going west to east it is often rappelled to reach the Klawatti Glacier at the point in the season that snow has melted down and a moat develops. Going east to west as the Terczaks were, it is an inevitable scramble up and over. While one approach could be to get one climber over the col, then belay the other(s) or haul packs, it is believed that most climbers make the approximate 150-foot scramble (depending on snow conditions) unroped.

At any rate, this unfortunate accident is consistent with North Cascades National Park SAR trends in that most mountaineers evacuated (ranging from non-critical immobilizing injuries to life-threatening trauma) get hurt in non-technical, but rugged terrain. The nature of accidents here seems to point to the greater hazards of carrying 50-pound mountaineering packs in steep exhausting terrain over the hazards of roped Class V climbing. (Source:

Kelly Bush, Wilderness District Ranger, North Cascades National Park)
*(Editor's Note: this was counted as two separate accidents in Tables II and III.)*

## FALL FROM A SNOW-COVERED BOULDER
### Washington, North Cascades National Park, Eldorado Peak

On July 18th, a party of four mountaineers were on approach to Eldorado Peak on the lower snow slopes of the Eldorado Glacier. While pausing on the upper side of a large rock outcrop, three of the men noticed that the fourth, Bill Stikker (57) had disappeared. They did not see him fall, but quickly found him unconscious at the base of the short rock cliff, an approximate 25-foot fall. The injured mountaineer was in good company, as two of his party are ER physicians and the third made impressive time descending the nearly 5000 feet to the road and driving to the ranger station in Marblemount to request help.

Further good fortune persisted as the NPS' contracted SAR helicopter happened to be at the ranger station and despite notification coming late in the day about this accident, rangers departed within the hour. Stikker was still unconscious and deteriorating. He was helicopter short-hauled from the accident site to a lower flat spot in Roush Creek basin, suitable for an Airlift NW medical helicopter to land. Rangers transferred him to flight medics who departed en route to Harborview Trauma Center, Seattle, just before dark. Mr. Stikker spent two weeks in the Neuro-ICU and an additional four weeks in hospital recovery before beginning outpatient therapy.

### Analysis

It is unknown how or why this climber fell from the snow-covered rock bluff that his partners had chosen as actually a good, safe spot to take a short rest stop. Again, the steep approaches to the routes of Cascade peaks can be the trouble spots. (Source: Kelly Bush, Wilderness District Ranger, North Cascades National Park)

## FALL ON SNOW, CLIMBING ALONE
### Washington, Mount Adams

On October 18, Derek Mamoyac (27) fell as he was descending after reaching Piker's Peak at 11,657 feet, below the mountain's summit. He stepped in some snow he thought was solid, but it gave way.

Mamoyac started up the 12,277-foot mountain Sunday for a one-day climb. Family members reported him missing Monday when he failed to show up for work.

After a five-day search, he was located just below the 6,000-foot level. He was taken by helicopter to a hospital in Portland. He was listed in fair condition. In addition to his fractured ankle, he was dehydrated and had swollen legs. He told rescuers he ate centipedes and drank water from creeks as he tried to crawl to safety.

## Analysis

Jill Bartlett and other rescuers spoke glowingly of Mamoyac after he was found alive after five frigid days and nights on the mountain. "He was in very good shape for what he went through," she told *The Oregonian*. As she and several other rescuers waited with him before he was flown from the mountain, he told them he ate centipedes and other bugs after running out of food early in the week. He drank water from creeks.

He was wearing water-resistant pants, insulated boots and gloves, but was still very cold. "We put all our coats on him, but he was still shivering," Bartlett said. "We asked him, 'Are you warm?' and he said, 'Yeah.'"

He spent nearly four days crawling and dragging his feet through the snow. When his knees hurt too much to crawl, he said he would turn around and scoot backward.

"We get happy endings, but not at the end of a five-day search," rescuer Varney said. (Source: From an Associated Press posting.)

## FALL ON ROCK, PROTECTION PULLED OUT
### West Virginia, Seneca Rocks

On October 11, Dr. Amy Ruth Stine (49) was killed in a fall at Seneca Rocks, a popular climbing spot in West Virginia. The climb she died on is a hard but short 5.9 that is G rated in the Barnes guide.

## Analysis

Although the facts are not completely clear, from the posts (on a rock-climbing.com thread) it sounds as if Amy was about 30 feet up the climb and had placed her second piece. She then fell and the piece she had just placed blew out, and the first piece was too low to prevent a big fall. She fell upside down and impacted her head and died instantly. She was wearing a helmet. (Source: from an article by Dayeen Rae Kurutz in the *Pittsburgh Tribune Review*, October 14, and a posting by Mitch Hyman)

## FALL ON ROCK
### West Virginia, New River Gorge, Central Endless Buttress, Kaymoor Slab

Early on the afternoon of November 1st, rangers received a report that a climber had been injured in a fall on the popular rock-climbing cliffs at Central Endless Wall. Rangers, EMS personnel, and members of the Fayette County vertical rescue team responded and found the victim—Nicholas Smith (21)—within an hour. He was found to be suffering from an apparent compound fractured leg. He had been lead climbing the 5.12-rated and bolted sport route known as "Pud's Pretty Dress" in the Kaymoor Slab area of the Central Endless Wall when he fell from a rock when about 60 feet up.

Smith's climbing rope caught him, but he swung out from the overhanging rock-face and struck a tree with his leg.

His belayer and climbing partners made a 911 call, then attended to his injuries until rescuers arrived. A technical hauling system was constructed and litter to the cliff top raised Smith. He was then flown to a hospital in Charleston. (Source: Frank Sellers, Park Ranger)

*(Editor's Note: It is likely that inadequate protection played a part in this incident. It is the only incident reported for 2008 from this popular climbing area.)*

## FALL ON ROCK, PROTECTION PULLED OUT
## Wisconsin, Devil's Lake State Park

In late May, a rock climber was rescued after falling about 40 feet. The 20-year-old man was taken by helicopter to University Hospital in Madison after he was stabilized by first-responders from Baraboo.

Authorities say the man and his girlfriend were climbing in an area above a trail Monday evening when he fell and suffered broken bones and other injuries.

Baraboo Ambulance Assistant Chief Kristine Snow said the accident is the first at Devil's Lake this year. Last year, ambulance workers were called to the park 18 times for rock-climbing injuries. (Source: From an article in the *Baraboo News Republic*)

*(Editor's Note: We have not been able to get incident data or narratives from Devil's Lake State Park in many years. It is obvious that there is a lot of climbing activity there with the number of responses needed. Our experience from the past tells us, however, that many—at least half—of the climbing-related callouts happen to individuals who were just scrambling about with no intention of climbing or being in a climbing situation.)*

## STRANDED — UNABLE TO FREE RAPPEL ROPE, WEATHER, HYPOTHERMIA
## Wyoming, Devil's Tower

On the evening of May 23rd, the park received a call from two stranded climbers (ages unknown) who were on the southwest face of the tower, asking for help. Aaron Turner and Travis Hubble were stranded one pitch down on the southwest rappel route, unable to pull their ropes from above due to a knot. The climbers had no headlamps, but were able to use the flash on their camera to help rescuers locate them. Due to lightning, thunder, fog and rain, though, it proved nearly impossible to determine their exact location. After communicating with Turner, climbing rangers learned that the two men had both ends of their rope and webbing material that could be used to make a Prusik to ascend their stuck ropes. Due to the hazardous conditions, the rangers determined that the safest and quickest way to facilitate a rescue would be to instruct Turner to ascend up his ropes to free the knot. Turner was able to free his rope, then descend to Hubble and pull the ropes down for the next rappel. The rangers found that Turner would then be able to rappel under his own power, but that Hubble was suffering from hypothermia and would need to be lowered with assistance from a climbing ranger via a tandem rappel. Both climbers safely reached the ground at 3:30 a.m. due to the expertise of the park's climbing rangers, law enforcement staff, and a local climbing guide. (Source: Dona Rutherford, Chief Ranger)

## FALL ON SNOW – UNABLE TO KICK STEPS, UNABLE TO SELF-ARREST (SOFT/ SLUSHY SNOW), FATIGUE
### Wyoming, Grand Teton National Park, Teewinot

On June 24 at 1000, I received a cell phone report from Exum Mountain Guide Christian Santelices, that a female (16) in a party of three had fallen on snow for about 100 meters and was injured. He told me that she had hip, ankle and elbow pain and multiple abrasions and lacerations. She did not lose consciousness but it was extremely painful for her to move and that wet snow avalanches were occurring in the area.

Rangers Motter and Feinberg were inserted to the accident site via short-haul. Ranger Byerly accompanying the litter and other rescue equipment was inserted on the second trip. The patient was then packaged on a vacuum mattress style backboard and placed in the litter. She was then flown, with Ranger Byerly attending, back to a waiting ambulance at the Lupine Meadows Rescue Cache and transported to St. John's Hospital in Jackson. Rangers Motter and Feinberg assisted the other members of the party off the mountain with the help of Mr. Santelices.

### Analysis

In a follow-up interview with the climber, she told me that before the fall she had been backing down the snow face in with crampons on and her ice ax in front of her. She felt comfortable and had recently refused an offer of a rope for protection. She told me that as she stepped down, a foothold in the snow gave way and she slipped. She was apparently descending in soft snow next to a rather deep runnel with a much firmer surface. When she fell, she tipped over backwards and began to cartwheel and tumble in the runnel. She said that she screamed when she realized that she was going over rocks. She attempted to self-arrest with her ice ax but was unsuccessful and let go of it when she thought she might become injured by it. She finally came to rest when she was able to jam her foot into some softer snow. Mr. Santelices reported that she was lucky to have stopped where she did given the even more treacherous terrain below her.

She had a lot of mountain experience for someone her age. *(Ed. Note: She considers herself moderately experienced.)* She had climbed multiple peaks in the Teton Range and had practiced extensively in the use of an ice ax. She was properly equipped for the climb and was wearing a helmet at the time of the accident. She was also reported to be the type that climbs within her abilities and asks for help when she needs it. Those of us that climb can all remember the time when we should have kicked that step a little deeper or sunk that axe a little harder. This young lady has learned a lesson that will help her through many years of mountaineering. (Source: Chris Harder)

*Further Notes from a report submitted by Erin Mauldin, the young lady who fell:*
"I should have been more careful on the descent. I was tired from having started at 12:30 that morning and was not kicking steps as seriously as I should have been. The snow was poor and I was just sliding into the previous footprints; it would have been better if I had placed my feet more carefully.

"Secondly, when I slipped, I should have kept a better grip on my ice ax. If I had had it in my hands and available, I might have been able to stop sooner by turning in and self-arresting. However, I think I made the best choice to let it go once I realized it was doing me no good.

"We still had crampons on because the area below the summit had been in shade and they had been useful on the way up and down that area. On the descent, there is a choice of going to the right or left of this rock face down two snow spits. Scott (56, climbing partner) chose the right (while facing in) and when the snow spit became narrow, he needed the crampons to cut steps. Ryan (c. 20, other climbing partner) and I crossed the rock face and descended the left and didn't really need the crampons. Once Scott met up with Ryan and I, we started post-holing, so it probably would have been a good idea to take the crampons off. We did not think of it at the time, especially since there were no good places to stop to take them off (mine are extremely old and lace up, so it requires some effort to do so).

"I was plunging the ice ax in vertically with each step. The snow in the area was all chewed up from Ryan's steps and ice ax and therefore not very solid. I might have made a faulty plunge when I slipped so that the ax came out easily or the snow was just soft and churned enough that it pulled right through. The leash was loose enough around my wrist that I was able to slip it off with my other hand.

Finally, the most important thing I did right was to wear a helmet. It saved me from severe injury and probably saved my life."

## FALL ON ROCK, CLIMBING ALONE, PROBABLE UNIQUE WEATHER EVENT
## Wyoming, Grand Teton National Park, Grand Teton, Lower Exum
On July 19, George Gardner (58) fell to his death while solo climbing the Lower Exum Ridge of the Grand Teton. Gardner and other Exum Guides were guiding youths from Wilderness Ventures, intending to climb the

Grand Teton on July 20th. After his clients had eaten and bedded down, Gardner asked Christian Santelices to attend to his clients and stated that he "was going for a walk for about an hour." Guides observed him walking toward the Lower Exum Ridge about 1700.

A major SAR operation ensued, involving about 20 rangers, three helitack crewmembers, and five of Gardner's fellow guides who were at the Lower Saddle with him. While guides searched for Gardner, several rangers flew by helicopter to Tepee Glacier and the Lower Saddle, initially to search for Gardner and then to recover his body after it was determined that he was deceased. His body was evacuated via helicopter long-line operation from the accident scene to the Lupine Meadows SAR Cache and then turned over to Teton County Coroner Bob Campbell. Several additional rangers provided emotional support to family and friends well into the evening.

**Analysis**

Although the exact circumstances of his accident never will be known, evidence suggests that he fell approximately 200 feet from the area just below the Black Face pitch at approximately 1800. His body was found in the gully to the west of the first pitch of the Lower Exum. A contributing factor may have been a sudden, near-60 mph wind gust that occurred at approximately 1745 and significantly exceeded the 40 mph winds that were prevalent at the Lower Saddle during the day.

George Gardner was an accomplished and seasoned mountaineer. He had been an Exum guide for 17 years and had climbed in the Teton Range for more than 20 years, holding certification as an AMGA Alpine Guide. His vast mountaineering experience included expeditions to the Southwest Face of Kanchenjunga in the Nepal Himalaya and the West Face of Hyani Potosi in Bolivia's Cordillera Real; ski descents in the Alps and in Colorado; and extensive climbing in North America. He had been the faculty member who originated the Sterling College (Vermont) "Mountain Cultures Semester".

It is common practice for Exum guides to hike or climb a nearby crag or peak while at the Lower Saddle after tending to their clients during Grand Teton guided trips. Whether or not a guide chooses to embark upon an early evening excursion is left entirely up to him/her.

The following points represent an outline of what is known about this particular accident:

- George Gardner set off from the Lower Saddle about 1700 on July 19, 2008, with the probable intention of soloing the Lower Exum Ridge route on the Grand Teton
- Based upon the physical evidence found on the body, he was wearing what one would be expected to have on for such an excursion; that is, light climbing clothing and very little in the way of additional equipment. He was wearing a climbing harness with a chalk bag, nearly-new 5.10 Gambit

rock climbing shoes, and had with him two, double-length nylon runners that he was carrying over one shoulder. These slings were doubled over and each was clipped to a carabiner.

- Gardner's body was located on the west side of the Lower Exum Ridge on a ledge situated beneath the pedestal from which the crux Black Face pitch is climbed.
- A blood smear/spatter was observed 20–30 feet up on the wall directly above the body. Gardner's hat was found on a ledge located about 100 feet above the body. This hat was known to be of the same type/color that he was known to wear. It had a cut in the material and what appeared to be blood and tissue on the inside of it.
- It appeared that Gardner had not moved after coming to rest on the ledge.
- The fall was obviously sufficient to sustain fatal injuries, but did not appear to be a particularly long fall because of the condition of the body.
- A noteworthy meteorological observation was logged by an NPS weather instrument that records data at a site located on the southern end of the Lower Saddle. The instrument logged winds of near-60 mph at about 1745 on the 19th.

The next statements/observations are speculative by nature. They are based upon a great deal of experience as well as the physical evidence:

- Although the exact circumstances of his accident never will be known, evidence suggests that he *may* have fallen approximately 200 feet, from the notch located just below the belay for the Black Rock Face pitch. If he had fallen from other locations below that point or higher up on the climb, his final resting place would have been substantially more to the east or west (or even on the south side of the climb), and his body would *likely* have demonstrated far more physical trauma.
- Additionally, it *may* have been Gardner's intention to have used the two double-length runners as a means to clip in to several of the fixed pitons that are to be found on the crux Black Face pitch. The crux pitch of the climb contains the climbing moves that are technically the most difficult. Sometimes, climbers will girth-hitch two longer runners to their harness so that they can clip (with carabiners) to resident, fixed protection as they climb up a particular pitch. As they move upwards and when they are clipped in to a particular piece, they are protected from a fall to a certain degree. This seems to be the only logical reason why Gardner had a climbing harness on in the first place. It suggests that since the runners were not in place, he had not reached the crux pitch.
- Because he left about 1700, it means that by 1745 he very likely could have been in the area of the notch at the base of the Black Rock Face. A contributing factor to his accident *may* have been a sudden near-60 mph

wind gust that occurred about this time and which significantly exceeded the 40 mph winds that were prevalent at the Lower Saddle during the day. If the unexpected near-60 mph wind gust had occurred while he was making difficult climbing moves, it *could have* contributed to his fall. (Source: From a report prepared by George J. Montopoli, Seasonal Park Ranger and Incident Commander, and Reynold G. Jackson, Jenny Lake Sub-District Ranger)

*(Editor's Note: The Exum Mountain Guide Service is reviewing its policy regarding the level and kinds of activities guides can participate in when clients are under their care.)*

## OVERDUE – CLIMBING ALONE, FALL ON SNOW,
### Wyoming, Grand Teton National Park, Avalanche Canyon

On August 5, Patty Felder contacted park dispatch to report that her husband, Richard Felder (58), was overdue from a descent of Avalanche Canyon. They had camped together in the South Fork of Cascade Canyon the previous evening, and in the morning, Ms. Felder hiked out via Cascade Canyon while her husband left to hike out via Avalanche Canyon.

A search was organized. On August 6 around 0930, searchers spotted Mr. Felder from Helicopter 20. Felder was at the base of a steep snowfield below Snowdrift Lake. He was waving a ski pole with one arm and appeared to be seriously injured. Rangers Vidak, Jernigan and Feinberg responded from Snowdrift Lake and arrived on scene about 15 minutes later. Their initial impression was that Mr. Felder had life-threatening injuries and rapid extrication was necessary. At 1735, Ranger Visnovske was short-hauled with a litter and medical gear from Lupine Meadows to the accident site. Mr. Felder was then packaged in the litter and short-hauled back to Lupine Meadows. He was then transferred to a waiting Medic 1 ambulance and transported to St. John's Hospital in Jackson.

All searchers in the field were then either flown back to the Rescue Cache or hiked out and returned to the Rescue Cache. A brief after action review was conducted and most personnel were released by 2130.

### Analysis

Mr. Felder had serious injuries and was flown to Memorial Herman Hospital in Houston, TX on August 8. Before he left, an interview was conducted. Though he was on heavy medications at the time of the interview, Mr. Felder gave the following account of his ordeal.

He said that the accident happened at about 0930 on August 5. He had hiked over Avalanche Divide and descended to Snowdrift Lake. Below the lake, he elected to get on a fairly steep snowfield to descend. He shortened his ski poles to use them as ice axes. He then slipped on the snow and managed to stop on a rock uninjured. At that point, he attempted to traverse the snow to a better location, but while doing so, broke through a hole in the snow and fell approximately ten feet, striking his head and landing in water. He then took a small rope from his pack and tied it to the pack and himself. Then he used his poles to cut steps in the snow to climb out. Once out of the hole, he hauled up his pack. While putting his pack on, he slipped again, dropping the pack. The pack slid down the snow and over about a ten-foot drop. Mr. Felder was still tied to the pack, so when it reached the end of the rope, he was jerked from his stance and fell approximately another 30 feet after his pack. (He likely sustained the serious injuries to his right arm, back, ribs and coccyx during this fall.) He again landed in water at the base of the snowfield but managed to quickly get up and out of the water. He lay down in the rocks about 30 feet from his pack and remained there unable to move for about the next 31 hours.

Mr. Felder said that he thought he had heard voices earlier in the morning, and Ranger Byerly said later that he had probably passed within 100 feet of where Mr. Felder lay while on his search up Avalanche Canyon. Mr. Felder was lying next to a very loud stream, so it would have been difficult for him to hear or be heard unless someone was very close. Mr. Felder also said that he had watched the helicopter fly over many times that day. He had wished that he could get to his pack to get out his yellow shirt to use to signal the helicopter.

*Some Conclusions:* While Mr. Felder chose to descend a non-trailed canyon that he knew little about, he did have a responsible party that knew where he was supposed to be and alerted rescue personnel in a timely manner. Had Mr. Felder been in Avalanche Canyon before, he may have known that it was possible to avoid the snow below Snowdrift Lake entirely by staying to the north side of the canyon. Once he had committed to traveling down the steep snow and suffered the head injury, he may not have been able to make the best of decisions. Being tied to his pack when it fell the second time certainly contributed to the most severe of his injuries. Mr. Felder was fortunate to have survived the night in only shorts and a T-shirt and most likely would not have survived a second night out.

Real credit for this successful rescue goes to the dedicated efforts of over 65 people from multiple agencies involved in the search. In a remote park with limited resources, Mr. Felder is fortunate that such a large and organized search effort was mounted with only about five hours to prepare. He is also fortunate to have received prompt and critical emergency care at St. John's Hospital. (Source: From a report submitted by Chris Harder, GTNP Ranger, and Grand Teton National Park News Releases, a website) *(Editor's Note: Here we have another hiker/ hiking accident that had some climb-*

*ing techniques involved. It is presented as an example of how hiking situations can result in needing climbing tools and techniques, especially if one is not familiar with the terrain.)*

### RAPPEL ERROR – FALL TO GROUND, UNFAMILIAR WITH EQUIPMENT
### Wyoming, Grand Teton National Park, Grand Teton

Around 1330 on August 7, Merry Carney (47) was unable to maintain her rappel, zipping down the rope approximately 50 feet to the ground. She had successfully climbed the Grand Teton by the Upper Exum Ridge with her husband, Pete, arriving at the summit at 1230. They then descended the Owen Spalding route, and she was on the lower 100-foot rappel to the Upper Saddle when she lost control.

Four rangers were flown to the Lower Saddle via a park contact helicopter, and two were inserted to the accident site just below the Upper Saddle (one at a time). M. Carney was medically assessed and fully immobilized onto a Benham backboard. She was then long-hauled back to Lupine Meadows with an attending ranger, arriving about 1645. She was transported to St. John's Hospital via park ambulance. As a result of her fall, M. Carney suffered five or six broken ribs and a tibia-fibula fracture of her lower right leg.

### Analysis

M. Carney was not wearing a helmet and certainly could have sustained a significant head injury had she become detached from the rappel rope and/ or not landed on her feet after plummeting about 50 feet.

The primary cause of this mishap is that for the first time in their mountaineering experiences, the Carneys were rappelling on two 8.2mm ropes using figure-eight devices. They had climbed the route previously (albeit some 25 years ago) and knew that the rappel involved about a 70-foot free-hanging section. A thicker rope, a better rappel setup, use of Prusiks or other self-belay setups on the rappel, or even preliminary practice rappelling with two 8.2-mm ropes, may have prevented this accident. (Source: From a report submitted by Chris Harder, GTNP Ranger)

### FALL ON SNOW – UNABLE TO SELF-ARREST, IMPROPER ICE AX TECHNIQUE
### Wyoming, Grand Teton National Park, Gilkey Tower

On August 9 about 1300, Chris Pazder (56) fell to his death while attempting to traverse from the South Teton to Cloudveil Dome. Pazder was in a climbing team of four who were traversing a snowfield on the south side of Gilkey Tower (about 12,320 feet), when the fall occurred. Pazder was the last climber in the party. When he slipped, he was unable to self-arrest, resulting in a fall of about 600-800 vertical feet. The climbing team was not roped at the time of the accident. All members were using an ice ax and wearing crampons.

A major SAR operation ensued, involving about twelve rangers and seven heli-tack crewmembers. An aerial reconnaissance helicopter flight was conducted with three rangers onboard to determine Pazder's location. Pazder was found in Avalanche Canyon at 1430. The aircrew was able to determine that he had sustained significant injuries from his fall and was deceased. A second team of rangers flew over the scene and verified the conclusions of the rangers on the original flight. Persistent thunderstorm activity and the lateness of the hour prevented further operations until the following day.

On August 10, a reconnaissance flight was conducted to determine the feasibility of inserting rangers directly to the accident scene and then extracting the victim from that location. The aircrew determined that that was not possible, so a ground-based recovery of Pazder's body followed. Six rangers were flown into Avalanche Canyon where they were able to climb to Pazder and then lower him to a location where he could be evacuated via helicopter long-line operation to Lupine Meadows. His body was flown to Lupine Meadows and was turned over to Teton County Coroner Bob Campbell.

### Analysis

In an attempt to document Chris Pazder's activities 24 hours prior to his death, the members of his climbing team—Jim Krudener, Michael Stiff, and Douglas Wales, all friends of his—were interviewed. The following narrative is the result of the interviews.

On Friday, August 8th about 1400, the climbing team left the Lupine Meadows trailhead and hiked to a camp in the South Fork of Garnet Canyon. They planned on climbing the South Teton (12,514 feet), then traversing east to Cloudveil Dome (12,026 feet), and then descending to their camp in Garnet Canyon to spend the night before hiking out to the Lupine Meadows trailhead on the morning of August 10th.

On August 9th about 0700, they left their camp in the South Fork to climb the South Teton, the first peak on their planned traverse. This involves climbing and descending the summits of the South Teton, Icecream Cone, the three summits of Gilkey Tower, then Spalding Peak and Cloudveil Dome. The traverse is long and complicated and requires constant diligence and route finding, though most parties belay only short sections. They reached the summit of the South Teton about 1000, and continued to the Icecream Cone (12,400 feet plus). Instead of climbing directly up the west side to the summit (rated 5.6), they traversed around the north side of the peak.

According to Jim Krudener, Pazder "...seemed OK on the N. side of the Icecream Cone, on belay on the ice section." The party continued towards Gilkey Tower, where they decided to traverse a snowfield on the south side of this peak. J. Krudener and M. Stiff stated that they elected to avoid the normal west ridge of Gilkey Tower because the ridge looked more difficult than they had expected, and the climbers didn't want to get the rope out. This ridge is rated Fourth Class in difficulty.

The snowfield appeared to be a faster and less complicated way to reach the Gilkey-Spalding Col, from which the party could ascend Spalding Peak and continue the traverse. They moved across the 30-35 degree snowfield unroped, with M. Stiff leading, followed by D. Wales, J. Krudener, and C. Pazder, respectively. The snow was not hard or icy. Wales described the snow as "very manageable—soft, but with firm purchase". Snow conditions were "mush", according to M. Stiff. The four climbers had removed their crampons after the traverse of Icecream Cone and decided to put them back on for this next snow crossing. They each had ice axes in their hands as they began to cross the snowfield.

The first three climbers crossed the snowfield and waited on a rock ledge as Pazder began crossing the snow. "He appeared to be calm and relaxed," according to J. Krudener. D. Wales stated that Pazder "...was 90 percent across. He was having fun and yelled at me to take his picture. I took it. He was in solid position and 30 seconds later when I was putting the camera away, I heard him yell. I saw him slide for about 20 feet and he disappeared behind the rocks still sliding."

Pazder was following in good steps and it is doubtful that "balling up" of snow in his crampons caused him to slip. It is noteworthy to mention that he was using rented crampons on lightweight (Tecnica) hiking boots at the time of the accident.

Digital photographs taken seconds before Pazder's fall show him swinging his ice ax from the handle, adze toward the slope. Pazder's use of the ax contrasts dramatically with that of the other three climbers. The others crossed the 30-35 degree snowfield with ice axes in the uphill hand, spike and shafts well driven into the snow. This *could* be an indication of Pazder's lack of competence with regard to ice ax technique. It also brings into question his ability and skill with regard to be able to instantly execute a self-arrest. According to M. Stiff, Pazder was "not using good ice ax technique" immediately prior to the accident.

Was Pazder too relaxed, and unaware of the consequences of a fall in this type of terrain? Mike Stiff related that, "He was perhaps not taking the terrain as seriously as he should have been." This *could* have been a factor in Pazder's fall, and *could* explain his unorthodox use of his ice ax just prior to his fall. In other words, was he using his ax in this fashion simply because he was hamming it up for the camera?

When a climber falls on a snow slope with big exposure, such as this one, it is imperative to execute a self-arrest immediately. Pazder seems to have had sufficient experience to cross this snowfield safely, and "he certainly had the experience to know what was required to self-arrest", according to M. Stiff. Chris Pazder had climbed on several steep snow slopes in Montana's Beartooth Mountains in the past ten years, and had climbed the Northwest Couloir on the South Teton in winter recently. M. Stiff said that Pazder "… knew how to use an ice ax".

We will never know [for sure] why Pazder was unable to arrest his fall. A small rock outcrop prevented his friends from seeing his entire initial slide. "He was out of view for a few seconds and when he reappeared, he was cart-wheeling," according to M. Stiff. The way that he was using his ice ax, swinging the adze into the slope, makes it much more difficult to go into an effective self-arrest position. Unfortunately, this translates to increasing velocity over time down the slope.

In closing, these observations may serve to prevent a similar accident.

- Familiarity and practice with the basic tools of mountaineering cannot be emphasized enough. The ability to self-arrest is crucial to snow travel in the mountains. An unchecked fall on steep snow can have dire consequences. One only needs to review the primary cause of mountaineering accidents in the Teton Range and around the world to have this point illustrated. The only way to acquire this skill is through practice.
- It is imperative that the climber be very focused while traveling in the mountain environment. While this may not have contributed to this accident, it serves as a reminder that a moment of inattention can have a terrible outcome.

Our thoughts are with Chris Pazder's family and friends as they struggle with this tremendous loss. (Source: From a report submitted by Chris Harder, GTNP Ranger)

## FALL ON ROCK, INADEQUATE BELAY – IMPROPER USE OF BELAY DEVICE
### Wyoming, Sinks Canyon, Killer Cave, Elmo's Fish

At 2:55 P.M. on November 23, Kelly Rush (29) fell from Elmo's Fish, a climb in the Killer Cave area of Sink's Canyon. She was on lead at the time and was not wearing a helmet.

Darran Wells, who was climbing nearby, said, "Stacy and I were between climbs on the right side of Killer Cave at the Main Wall in Sinks Canyon. We heard a loud crash followed by screams from about 200 yards South along the main wall (climbers left of Killer Cave.) I ran there to find [the patient] lying on her back on uneven rocky terrain at the base of Elmo's Fish. She was still tied into the rope and had apparently fallen from 20 to 25 feet and landed in the position I found her (on her back with her head hanging off the edge of the rock). I immediately stabilized her head and asked her not to move until we could determine if she had injured her back. At that point, I yelled across the cave for someone to call 911. She was alert and oriented (A&0x4) and denied any loss of consciousness. She had two friends with her (including the belayer) who were both visibly shaken up and standing nearby. She had apparently bitten her tongue on impact and blood was coming from her mouth. She complained of lower back pain and said that she had taken a lead fall near the third bolt.

About that time, Andy Blair (thankfully) arrived and began a thorough patient assessment and vitals while I maintained cervical spinal immobilization. Chris Agnew arrived just after Andy and wrote a complete SOAP note as Andy was taking vitals. After a few minutes, a woman (who's name I forget) arrived who said she was a PA at the hospital. Several others arrived to help. After Andy did a full patient assessment, a group of six of us lifted and moved her (BEAM technique) off the uneven rocks and onto a foam pad on the trail. We covered her with coats to keep her warm. After a third or fourth set of vitals, Deb (EMT) arrived with $O_2$ followed by SAR and Fire dept and Sheriff's office personnel with a stokes litter and wheel. Deb applied a neck brace and supervised moving Kelly onto a backboard. Andy administered $O_2$ with a nasal cannula, and we moved her into a Stokes Litter with a single wheel for transport down the hill to the ambulance. Kelly remained conscious and in good spirits throughout."

Word on the street was that Kelly was discharged from the hospital the same night with no major injuries.

**Analysis**

Stacy talked directly with the woman who was belaying Kelly at the time of the fall. The belayer said she was grabbing the Grigri to pay out slack at the time that Kelly fell. She did not have a hand on the brake. When Kelly fell, she did not have the presence of mind to release the Grigri, so without a hand on the brake line, the rope just sailed through the device.

This is not a new problem, but certainly a critically important one for belayers using a Grigri to be aware of. (Source: Darran Wells and John Gookin)

# STATISTICAL TABLES

## TABLE I
## REPORTED MOUNTAINEERING ACCIDENTS

| | Number of Accidents Reported | | Total Persons Involved | | Injured | | Fatalities | |
|---|---|---|---|---|---|---|---|---|
| | USA | CAN | USA | CAN | USA | CAN | USA | CAN |
| 1951 | 15 | | 22 | | 11 | | 3 | |
| 1952 | 31 | | 35 | | 17 | | 13 | |
| 1953 | 24 | | 27 | | 12 | | 12 | |
| 1954 | 31 | | 41 | | 31 | | 8 | |
| 1955 | 34 | | 39 | | 28 | | 6 | |
| 1956 | 46 | | 72 | | 54 | | 13 | |
| 1957 | 45 | | 53 | | 28 | | 18 | |
| 1958 | 32 | | 39 | | 23 | | 11 | |
| 1959 | 42 | 2 | 56 | 2 | 31 | 0 | 19 | 2 |
| 1960 | 47 | 4 | 64 | 12 | 37 | 8 | 19 | 4 |
| 1961 | 49 | 9 | 61 | 14 | 45 | 10 | 14 | 4 |
| 1962 | 71 | 1 | 90 | 1 | 64 | 0 | 19 | 1 |
| 1963 | 68 | 11 | 79 | 12 | 47 | 10 | 19 | 2 |
| 1964 | 53 | 11 | 65 | 16 | 44 | 10 | 14 | 3 |
| 1965 | 72 | 0 | 90 | 0 | 59 | 0 | 21 | 0 |
| 1966 | 67 | 7 | 80 | 9 | 52 | 6 | 16 | 3 |
| 1967 | 74 | 10 | 110 | 14 | 63 | 7 | 33 | 5 |
| 1968 | 70 | 13 | 87 | 19 | 43 | 12 | 27 | 5 |
| 1969 | 94 | 11 | 125 | 17 | 66 | 9 | 29 | 2 |
| 1970 | 129 | 11 | 174 | 11 | 88 | 5 | 15 | 5 |
| 1971 | 110 | 17 | 138 | 29 | 76 | 11 | 31 | 7 |
| 1972 | 141 | 29 | 184 | 42 | 98 | 17 | 49 | 13 |
| 1973 | 108 | 6 | 131 | 6 | 85 | 4 | 36 | 2 |
| 1974 | 96 | 7 | 177 | 50 | 75 | 1 | 26 | 5 |
| 1975 | 78 | 7 | 158 | 22 | 66 | 8 | 19 | 2 |
| 1976 | 137 | 16 | 303 | 31 | 210 | 9 | 53 | 6 |
| 1977 | 121 | 30 | 277 | 49 | 106 | 21 | 32 | 11 |
| 1978 | 118 | 17 | 221 | 19 | 85 | 6 | 42 | 10 |
| 1979 | 100 | 36 | 137 | 54 | 83 | 17 | 40 | 19 |
| 1980 | 191 | 29 | 295 | 85 | 124 | 26 | 33 | 8 |
| 1981 | 97 | 43 | 223 | 119 | 80 | 39 | 39 | 6 |
| 1982 | 140 | 48 | 305 | 126 | 120 | 43 | 24 | 14 |
| 1983 | 187 | 29 | 442 | 76 | 169 | 26 | 37 | 7 |
| 1984 | 182 | 26 | 459 | 63 | 174 | 15 | 26 | 6 |
| 1985 | 195 | 27 | 403 | 62 | 190 | 22 | 17 | 3 |
| 1986 | 203 | 31 | 406 | 80 | 182 | 25 | 37 | 14 |

| | Number of Accidents Reported | | Total Persons Involved | | Injured | | Fatalities | |
|---|---|---|---|---|---|---|---|---|
| | USA | CAN | USA | CAN | USA | CAN | USA | CAN |
| 1987 | 192 | 25 | 377 | 79 | 140 | 23 | 32 | 9 |
| 1988 | 156 | 18 | 288 | 44 | 155 | 18 | 24 | 4 |
| 1989 | 141 | 18 | 272 | 36 | 124 | 11 | 17 | 9 |
| 1990 | 136 | 25 | 245 | 50 | 125 | 24 | 24 | 4 |
| 1991 | 169 | 20 | 302 | 66 | 147 | 11 | 18 | 6 |
| 1992 | 175 | 17 | 351 | 45 | 144 | 11 | 43 | 6 |
| 1993 | 132 | 27 | 274 | 50 | 121 | 17 | 21 | 1 |
| 1994 | 158 | 25 | 335 | 58 | 131 | 25 | 27 | 5 |
| 1995 | 168 | 24 | 353 | 50 | 134 | 18 | 37 | 7 |
| 1996 | 139 | 28 | 261 | 59 | 100 | 16 | 31 | 6 |
| 1997 | 158 | 35 | 323 | 87 | 148 | 24 | 31 | 13 |
| 1998 | 138 | 24 | 281 | 55 | 138 | 18 | 20 | 1 |
| 1999 | 123 | 29 | 248 | 69 | 91 | 20 | 17 | 10 |
| 2000 | 150 | 23 | 301 | 36 | 121 | 23 | 24 | 7 |
| 2001 | 150 | 22 | 276 | 47 | 138 | 14 | 16 | 2 |
| 2002 | 139 | 27 | 295 | 29 | 105 | 23 | 34 | 6 |
| 2003 | 118 | 29 | 231 | 32 | 105 | 22 | 18 | 6 |
| 2004 | 160 | 35 | 311 | 30 | 140 | 16 | 35 | 14 |
| 2005 | 111 | 19 | 176 | 41 | 85 | 14 | 34 | 7 |
| 2006 | 109 | | 227 | | 89 | | 21 | |
| 2007 | 113 | | 211 | | 95 | | 15 | |
| 2008 | 112 | | 203 | | 96 | | 19 | |
| Totals | 6,445 | 958 | 11,739 | 2003 | 5,438 | 715 | 1,428 | 292 |

# TABLE II

| Geographical Districts | 1951–2007 | | | 2008 | | |
|---|---|---|---|---|---|---|
| | Number of Accidents | Deaths | Total Persons Involved | Number of Accidents | Deaths | Total Persons Involved |
| **CANADA*** | | | | | | |
| Alberta | 520 | 142 | 1033 | | | |
| British Columbia | 317 | 119 | 641 | | | |
| Yukon Territory | 37 | 28 | 77 | | | |
| New Brunswick | 1 | 0 | 0 | | | |
| Ontario | 37 | 9 | 67 | | | |
| Quebec | 31 | 10 | 63 | | | |
| East Arctic | 8 | 2 | 21 | | | |
| West Arctic | 2 | 2 | 2 | | | |
| Practice Cliffs[1] | 20 | 2 | 36 | | | |
| **UNITED STATES** | | | | | | |
| Alaska | 513 | 188 | 870 | 13 | 4 | 19 |
| Arizona, Nevada Texas | 93 | 18 | 170 | 2 | 0 | 2 |
| Atlantic–North | 977 | 148 | 1680 | 27 | 2 | 53 |
| Atlantic–South | 107 | 25 | 186 | 11 | 2 | 21 |
| California | 1286 | 295 | 2553 | 19 | 1 | 32 |
| Central | 135 | 18 | 218 | 1 | 0 | 1 |
| Colorado | 767 | 213 | 2308 | 12 | 3 | 23 |
| Montana, Idaho South Dakota | 83 | 32 | 134 | 1 | 1 | 1 |
| Oregon | 207 | 111 | 471 | 4 | 1 | 10 |
| Utah, New Mexico | 167 | 59 | 309 | 8 | 1 | 13 |
| Washington | 1043 | 319 | **882 | ***7 | 2 | 16 |
| Wyoming | 562 | 131 | 1014 | 7 | 2 | 12 |

\* No reports from 2006–2008
\*\* This number was incorrect last year. It should have been 867, not 16.
\*\*\* In a party of two, one accident happened on the ascent and the second accident happened to the deceased's climbing partner on the descent.

[1]This category includes bouldering, artificial climbing walls, buildings, and so forth. These are also added to the count of each province, but not to the total count, though that error has been made in previous years. The Practice Cliffs category has been removed from the U.S. data.

## TABLE III

| | 1951–07 USA | 1959–05 CAN. | 2008 USA | 2008 CAN. |
|---|---|---|---|---|
| **Terrain** | | | | |
| Rock | 4453 | 528 | 77 | |
| Snow | 2336 | 355 | 31 | |
| Ice | 267 | 15 | 3 | |
| River | 14 | 3 | 1 | |
| Unknown | 22 | 10 | 0 | |
| **Ascent or Descent** | | | | |
| Ascent | 2994 | 587 | 82 | |
| Descent | 2273 | 371 | 29 | |
| Unknown | 249 | 13 | 1 | |
| OtherN.B. | 7 | 0 | 0 | |
| **Immediate Cause** | | | | |
| Fall or slip on rock | 3522 | 290 | 67 | |
| Slip on snow or ice | 1010 | 207 | 13 | |
| Falling rock, ice, or object | 623 | 137 | 3 | |
| Exceeding abilities | 547 | 32 | 3 | |
| Illness[1] | 391 | 26 | 9 | |
| Stranded | 339 | 53 | 6 | |
| Avalanche | 289 | 127 | 5 | |
| Rappel Failure/Error2 | 291 | 47 | 6 | |
| Exposure | 272 | 14 | 3 | |
| Loss of control/glissade | 207 | 17 | 4 | |
| Nut/chock pulled out | 220 | 9 | 16 | |
| Failure to follow route | 186 | 30 | 2 | |
| Fall into crevasse/moat | 163 | 50 | 2 | |
| Faulty use of crampons | 107 | 6 | 2 | |
| Piton/ice screw pulled out | 95 | 13 | 0 | |
| Ascending too fast | 66 | 0 | 0 | |
| Skiing[3] | 56 | 11 | 0 | |
| Lightning | 46 | 7 | 0 | |
| Equipment failure | 15 | 3 | 0 | |
| Other[4] | 466 | 37 | 25 | |
| Unknown | 61 | 10 | 0 | |
| **Contributory Causes** | | | | |
| Climbing unroped | 1007 | 165 | 6 | |
| Exceeding abilities | 905 | 202 | 10 | |
| Placed no/inadequate protection | 736 | 96 | 26 | |
| Inadequate equipment/clothing | 683 | 70 | 7 | |
| Weather | 471 | 67 | 8 | |
| Climbing alone | 397 | 69 | 7 | |
| No hard hat | 343 | 71 | 5 | |

| | 1951–07 USA | 1959–05 CAN | 2008 USA | 2008 CAN |
|---|---|---|---|---|
| **Contributory Causes (continued)** | | | | |
| Inadequate belay | 209 | 28 | 9 | |
| Nut/chock pulled out | 200 | 32 | 1 | |
| Poor position | 177 | 20 | 8 | |
| Darkness | 141 | 21 | 5 | |
| Party separated | 117 | 12 | 0 | |
| Failure to test holds | 101 | 32 | 0 | |
| Piton/ice screw pulled out | 86 | 13 | 0 | |
| Failed to follow directions | 73 | 12 | 0 | |
| Exposure | 64 | 16 | 0 | |
| Illness1 | 40 | 9 | 0 | |
| Equipment failure | 11 | 7 | 0 | |
| Other[4] | 264 | 100 | 4 | |
| Age of Individuals | | | | |
| Under 15 | 1245 | 12 | 1 | |
| 15–20 | 1271 | 203 | 10 | |
| 21–25 | 1407 | 257 | 13 | |
| 26–30 | 1288 | 211 | 15 | |
| 31–35 | 1080 | 114 | 13 | |
| 36–50 | 1237 | 143 | 30 | |
| Over 50 | 247 | 31 | 23 | |
| Unknown | 1977 | 530 | 25 | |
| Experience Level | | | | |
| None/Little | 1768 | 304 | 9 | |
| Moderate (1 to 3 years) | 1619 | 354 | 16 | |
| Experienced | 1974 | 440 | 65 | |
| Unknown | 2045 | 559 | 38 | |
| Month of Year | | | | |
| January | 229 | 25 | 7 | |
| February | 210 | 55 | 0 | |
| March | 307 | 68 | 8 | |
| April | 407 | 39 | 3 | |
| May | 918 | 62 | 20 | |
| June | 1060 | 70 | 21 | |
| July | 1134 | 254 | 20 | |
| August | 1046 | 184 | 11 | |
| September | 1179 | 75 | 5 | |
| October | 454 | 42 | 12 | |
| November | 194 | 20 | 5 | |
| December | 100 | 24 | 0 | |
| Unknown | 17 | 1 | 0 | |

| | 1951–07 USA | 1959–05 CAN | 2008 USA | 2008 CAN |
|---|---|---|---|---|
| **Type of Injury/Illness (Data since 1984)** | | | | |
| Fracture | 1259 | 223 | 44 | |
| Laceration | 703 | 71 | 17 | |
| Abrasion | 339 | 76 | 9 | |
| Bruise | 479 | 83 | 27 | |
| Sprain/strain | 350 | 33 | 22 | |
| Concussion | 235 | 28 | 12 | |
| Hypothermia | 156 | 16 | 4 | |
| Frostbite | 125 | 12 | 7 | |
| Dislocation | 125 | 16 | 0 | |
| Puncture | 45 | 13 | 0 | |
| Acute Mountain Sickness | 44 | 0 | 1 | |
| HAPE | 72 | 0 | 1 | |
| HACE | 25 | 0 | 0 | |
| Other[5] | 323 | 49 | 8 | |
| None | 239 | 188 | 9 | |

N.B. Some accidents happen when climbers are at the top or bottom of a route, not climbing. They may be setting up a belay or rappel or are just not anchored when they fall. (This category created in 2001. The category unknown is primarily because of solo climbers.)

[1]These illnesses/injuries, which led directly or indirectly to the accident, include: AMS; HAPE and possible CO poisoning; frostbite (3); fatigue (6); collapsed and died on Denali (2) one on summit and another on descent; Raynaud's disease.

[2]These include: rappelled off the end of the rope, uneven ropes, mistook 5m (1) and 20 m mark (1) mark for middle of rope; did not attach second rappel rope to anchor; used 8.2 mm rope w/figure-8; threaded lowering rope through nylon webbing sling; and lowering errors (5).

[3]This category was set up originally for ski mountaineering. Backcountry touring or snow-shoeing incidents—even if one gets avalanched—are not in the data.

[4]These included: automatically using same site w/out checking conditions (avalanche); failure to turn back—led to frostbite; rapid weather change; removing gloves in cold; unable to self-arrest (5); relied on old webbing for rappel anchor; knee stuck in crack (2); late start; improper use of ascenders (severed rope); fall in river on descent; inappropriate technique—including putting finger in bolt eye (3); miscommunication between climber and belayer; rope severed on jagged rocks; distraction—talking to others while setting up rappel; rappel rope stuck in crack; handhold dislodged—rock fell on climbing partner; inexperienced belayer; late start.

[5]These included: dehydration (2); subdural hematoma (hence ICP); rope burns to hands; pneumothorax (2).

*(Editor's Note: Under the category "other," many of the particular items will have been recorded under a general category. For example, the climber who dislodges a rock that falls on another climber would be coded as Falling Rock/Object. A climber who has a hand or foot-hold come loose and falls would be coded as Fall On Rock and Other – and most often includes Failure To Test Holds.)*

# MOUNTAIN RESCUE UNITS IN NORTH AMERICA
**Denotes team fully certified—Technical Rock,
Snow & Ice, Wilderness Search;
S, R, SI = certified partially in Search, Rock, and/or Snow & Ice

## ALASKA
**Alaska Mountain Rescue Group.** PO Box 241102, Anchorage,
AK 99524. www.amrg.org

**Denali National Park SAR.** PO Box 588, Talkeetna, AK 99676.
Dena_talkeetna@nps.gov

**Juneau Mountain Rescue, Inc.** 2970 Foster Ave., Juneau, AK 99801

**Sitka Mountain Search and Rescue.** 209 Lake St., Sitka, AK 99835

**US Army Alaskan Warfare Training Center.** #2900 501 Second St., APO AP 96508

## ARIZONA
**Apache Rescue Team.** PO Box 100, St. Johns, AZ 85936

**Arizona Department Of Public Safety Air Rescue.** Phoenix, Flagstaff, Tucson,
Kingman, AZ

**Arizona Division Of Emergency Services.** Phoenix, AZ

**Grand Canyon National Park Rescue Team.** PO Box 129, Grand Canyon, AZ 86023

**Central Arizona Mountain Rescue Team/Maricopa County Sheriff's Office
MR.** PO Box 4004 Phoenix, AZ 85030. www.mcsomr.org

**Sedona Fire District Special Operations Rescue Team.** 2860 Southwest Dr.,
Sedona, AZ 86336. ropes@sedona.net

**Southern Arizona Rescue Assn**/Pima County Sheriff's Office. PO Box 12892,
Tucson, AZ 85732. http://hambox.theriver.com/sarci/sara01.html

## CALIFORNIA
**Altadena Mountain Rescue Team.** 780 E. Altadena Dr., Altadena, CA 91001
www.altadenasheriffs.org/rescue/amrt.html

**Bay Area Mountain Rescue Team.** PO Box 19184, Stanford, CA 94309 bamru@
hooked.net

**California Office of Emergency Services.** 2800 Meadowview Rd., Sacramento, CA.
95832. warning.center@oes.ca.gov

**China Lake Mountain Rescue Group.** PO Box 2037, Ridgecrest, CA 93556
www.clmrg.org

**Inyo County Sheriff's Posse SAR.** PO Box 982, Bishop, CA 93514
inyocosar@juno.com

**Joshua Tree National Park SAR.** 74485 National Monument Drive,
Twenty Nine Palms, CA 92277. patrick_suddath@nps.gov

**Malibu Mountain Rescue Team.** PO Box 222, Malibu, CA 90265.
www.mmrt.org

**Montrose SAR Team.** PO Box 404, Montrose, CA 91021

**Riverside Mountain Rescue Unit.** PO Box 5444, Riverside,
CA 92517. www.rmru.org  rmru@bigfoot.com

**San Bernardino County Sheriff's Cave Rescue Team.** 655 E. Third St.
San Bernardino, CA 92415
www.sbsd-vfu.org/units/SAR/SAR203/sar203_1.htm

**San Bernardino County So/ West Valley SAR.** 13843 Peyton Dr., Chino Hills, CA 91709.

**San Diego Mountain Rescue Team.** PO Box 81602, San Diego, CA 92138. www.sdmrt.org

**San Dimas Mountain Rescue Team.** PO Box 35, San Dimas, CA 91773

**Santa Barbara SAR Team.** PO Box 6602, Santa Barbara, CA 93160-6602

**Santa Clarita Valley SAR / L.A.S.O.** 23740 Magic Mountain Parkway, Valencia, CA 91355. http://members.tripod.com/scvrescue/

Sequoia-Kings Canyon National Park Rescue Team. Three Rivers, CA 93271

**Sierra Madre SAR.** PO Box 24, Sierra Madre, CA 91025. www.mra.org/smsrt.html

**Ventura County SAR.** 2101 E. Olson Rd, Thousand Oaks, CA 91362 www.vcsar.org

Yosemite National Park Rescue Team. PO Box 577-SAR, Yosemite National Park, CA 95389

## COLORADO

**Alpine Rescue Team.** PO Box 934, Evergreen, CO 80437 www.alpinerescueteam.org

Colorado Ground SAR. 2391 Ash St, Denver, CO 80222 www.coloradowingcap.org/CGSART/Default.htm

**Crested Butte SAR.** PO Box 485, Crested Butte, CO 81224

Douglas County Search And Rescue. PO Box 1102, Castle Rock, CO 80104. www.dcsarco.org info@dcsarco.org

**El Paso County SAR.** 3950 Interpark Dr, Colorado Springs, CO 80907-9028. www.epcsar.org

Eldorado Canyon State Park. PO Box B, Eldorado Springs, CO 80025

**Grand County SAR.** Box 172, Winter Park, CO 80482

**Larimer County SAR.** 1303 N. Shields St., Fort Collins, CO 80524. www.fortnet. org/LCSAR/ lcsar@co.larimer.co.us

**Mountain Rescue Aspen.** 630 W. Main St, Aspen, CO 81611 www.mountainrescueaspen.org

Park County SAR, CO. PO Box 721, Fairplay, CO 80440

Rocky Mountain National Park Rescue Team. Estes Park, CO 80517

**Rocky Mountain Rescue Group.** PO Box Y, Boulder, CO 80306 www.colorado.edu/StudentGroups/rmrg/ rmrg@colorado.edu

Routt County SAR. PO Box 772837, Steamboat Springs, CO 80477 RCSAR@co.routt.co.us

**Summit County Rescue Group.** PO Box 1794, Breckenridge, CO 80424

**Vail Mountain Rescue Group.** PO Box 1597, Vail, CO 81658 http://sites.netscape.net/vailmra/homepage vmrg@vail.net

**Western State College Mountain Rescue Team.** Western State College Union, Gunnison, CO 81231. org_mrt@western.edu

## IDAHO

**Bonneville County SAR.** 605 N. Capital Ave, Idaho Falls, ID 83402 www.srv.net/~jrcase/bcsar.html

**Idaho Mountain SAR.** PO Box 741, Boise, ID 83701. www.imsaru.org rsksearch@aol.com

## MAINE
**Acadia National Park SAR.** Bar Harbor, Maine

## MARYLAND
**\*\*Maryland Sar Group.** 5434 Vantage Point Road, Columbia, MD 21044
Peter_McCabe@Ed.gov

## MONTANA
**Glacier National Park SAR.** PO Box 128, Glacier National Park,
West Glacier, MT 59936
**Flathead County Search and Rescue.** 920 South Main St., Kalispell, MT 59901.
Sheriff's Office phone: 406-758-5585.

## NEVADA
**\*\*Las Vegas Metro PD SAR.** 4810 Las Vegas Blvd., South Las Vegas,
NV 89119. www.lvmpdsar.com

## NEW MEXICO
**\*\*Albuquerque Mountain Rescue Council.** PO Box 53396, Albuquerque,
NM 87153. www.abq.com/amrc/ albrescu@swcp.com

## NEW HAMPSHIRE
**Appalachian Mountain Club.** Pinkham Notch Camp, Gorham, NH 03581
**Mountain Rescue Service.** PO Box 494, North Conway, NH 03860

## NEW YORK
**76 SAR.** 243 Old Quarry Rd., Feura Bush, NY 12067
**Mohonk Preserve Rangers.** PO Box 715, New Paltz, NY 12561
**NY State Forest Rangers.** 50 Wolf Rd., Room 440C, Albany, NY 12233

## OREGON
**\*\*Corvallis Mountain Rescue Unit.** PO Box 116, Corvallis, OR 97339
www.cmrv.peak.org
**(S, R) Deschutes County SAR.** 63333 West Highway 20, Bend, OR 97701
**\*\*Eugene Mountain Rescue.** PO Box 20, Eugene, OR 97440
**\*\*Hood River Crag Rats Rescue Team.** 2880 Thomsen Rd., Hood River,
OR 97031
**\*\*Portland Mountain Rescue.** PO Box 5391, Portland, OR 97228
www.pmru.org info@pmru.org

## PENNSYLVANNIA
**\*\*Allegheny Mountain Rescue Group.** c/o Mercy Hospital,
1400 Locust, Pittsburgh, PA 15219. www.asrc.net/amrg
**\*\*Wilderness Emergency Strike Team.** 11 North Duke Street, Lancaster,
PA 17602. www.west610.org

## UTAH
**\*\*Davis County Sheriff's SAR.** PO Box 800, Farmington, UT 84025
www.dcsar.org

**Rocky Mountain Rescue Dogs.** 3353 S. Main #122, Salt Lake City, UT 84115
**\*\*Salt Lake County Sheriff's SAR.** 3510 South 700 West, Salt Lake City, UT 84119
**San Juan County Emergency Services.** PO Box 9, Monticello, UT 84539
**\*\*Utah County Sherrif's SAR.** PO Box 330, Provo, UT 84603.
   ucsar@utah.uswest.net
**\*\*Weber County Sheriff's Mountain Rescue.** 745 Nancy Dr, Ogden,
   UT 84403. http://planet.weber.edu/mru
**Zion National Park SAR.** Springdale, UT 84767

## VERMONT
**\*\*Stowe Mountain Rescue.** P.O. Box 291, Stowe, VT 05672
   www.stowevt.org/htt/

## VIRGINIA
**Air Force Rescue Coordination Center.** Suite 101, 205 Dodd Building,
   Langley AFB, VA 23665. www2.acc.af.mil/afrcc/airforce.rescue@usa.net

## WASHINGTON STATE
**\*\*Bellingham Mountain Rescue Council.** PO Box 292, Bellingham, WA 98225
**\*\*Central Washington Mountain Rescue Council.** PO Box 2663, Yakima, WA
   98907. www.nwinfo.net/~cwmr/ cwmr@nwinfo.net
**\*\*Everett Mountain Rescue Unit, Inc.** 5506 Old Machias Road, Snohomish, WA
   98290-5574. emrui@aol.com
**Mount Rainier National Park Rescue Team.** Longmire, WA 98397
**North Cascades National Park Rescue Team.** 728 Ranger Station Rd,
   Marblemount, WA 98267
**\*\*Olympic Mountain Rescue.** PO Box 4244, Bremerton, WA 98312
   www.olympicmountainrescue.org information@olympicmountainrescue.org
**Olympic National Park Rescue Team.** 600 Park Ave, Port Angeles, WA 98362
**\*\*Seattle Mountain Rescue.** PO Box 67, Seattle, WA 98111
   www.eskimo.com/~pc22/SMR/smr.html
**\*\*Skagit Mountain Rescue.** PO Box 2, Mt. Vernon, WA 98273
**\*\*Tacoma Mountain Rescue.** PO Box 696, Tacoma, WA 98401
   www.tmru.org
**North Country Volcano Rescue Team.** 404 S. Parcel Ave, Yacolt, WA 98675
   www.northcountryems.org/vrt/index.html

## WASHINGTON, DC
**National Park Service, EMS/SAR Division.** Washington, DC
**US Park Police Aviation.** Washington, DC

## WYOMING
**Grand Teton National Park Rescue Team.** PO Box 67, Moose, WY 83012
**Park County SAR, WY.** Park County SO, 1131 11th, Cody, WY 82412

## CANADA
**North Shore Rescue Team.** 147 E. 14th St, North Vancouver, B.C.,
   Canada V7L 2N4
**\*\*Rocky Mountain House SAR.** Box 1888, Rocky Mountain House, Alberta,
   Canada T0M 1T0

# MOUNTAIN RESCUE ASSOCIATION
www.mra.org

Charley Shimanski, President
Alpine Rescue Team CO
67 Pauls Road, Evergreen, CO 80439
president@mra.org
303-832-5710 (w)   303-909-9348 (cell)
Term Expires June 2010

Neil Van Dyke, Vice President
Stowe Mountain Rescue, VT
PO Box 291, Stowe, VT 05672
vp@mra.org
802-253-9060
Term Expires June 2010

Dan Land, Secretary/Treasurer
San Dimas Mountain Rescue Team, CA
PO Box 35, San Dimas, CA 91773
sectreas@mra.org
909 621-9988 (h)   909-268-2237 (cell)
Term Expires 2009

Doug Wessen, Member-at-Large
Juneau Mountain Rescue, Inc., AK
2970 Foster Ave., Juneau, AK 99801
dougwessen@gmail.com
907-586-4834
Term Expires 2010

Mike Vorachek, Member-at-Large
Bonneville County SAR, ID
2125 Brentwood Dr., Idaho Falls, ID 83402
mtnsar@cableone.net
208-553-5724 (w)   208-521-6882 (cell)
Term Expires 2009

Kayley Trujillo, Executive Secretary
PO Box 880868, San Diego, CA 92168
info@mra.org
858-229-4295 (h)   951-317-5635 (cell)